# WHEN I PUT OUT TO SEA

# WHEN I PUT

5D STEIN AND DAY/*Publishers*/NewYork

# OUT TO SEA

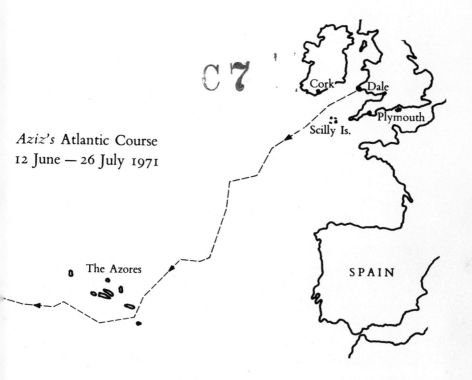

*Aziz's* Atlantic Course
12 June — 26 July 1971

Cork   Dale

Plymouth

Scilly Is.

The Azores

SPAIN

## NICOLETTE MILNES WALKER

First published in 1972
Copyright © Nicolette Milnes Walker 1972
Library of Congress Catalog Card No. 76-187101
All rights reserved
Designed by David Miller
Printed in the United States of America
Stein and Day/Publishers/7 East 48 Street, New York, N.Y. 10017
ISBN 0-8128-1467-3

# Contents

ACKNOWLEDGMENTS

The author is grateful to Elizabeth Jennings for permission to print her poem *Power;* and to the Trustees of the Estate of the late James Elroy Flecker, and William Heinemann Limited, for their permission to use two stanzas from *Hassan.*

We are the Pilgrims, master; we shall go
    Always a little further: it may be
Beyond that last blue mountain barred with snow
    Across that angry or that glimmering sea,

White on a throne or guarded in a cave
    There lives a prophet who can understand
Why men were born: but surely we are brave,
    Who take the Golden Road to Samarkand.
              From *Hassan**
              By James Elroy Flecker

* By permission of the Estate of the late James Elroy Flecker and William Heinemann Ltd.

The *New York Times*, Tuesday, July 27, 1971

## First Woman Sails Sloop
## Nonstop Across Atlantic

*Newport, R.I.*, July 26 (AP) —a 28-year-old British psychologist brought her 30-foot sloop to port today and became the first woman to sail nonstop across the Atlantic Ocean.

Nicolette Milnes Walker stepped ashore after her 45-day, 3,500 mile trip and said she wanted a bath, a steak and sleep. She left Dale, Wales, on June 12.

# ONE

# Why?

On June 12, 1971, I climbed into my sailboat prepared to flee. I was about to escape from a world that no longer gave me comfort or joy, from a job that bored me, and a love affair that was doomed. I wanted out.

Nearly everyone, at some time, is tempted to escape from his life. Some people flee into insanity. Some make a physical assault on themselves, or on others. My way out was not so extreme. I was going to sail the Atlantic Ocean single-handed.

I was going to flirt with death, with insanity, with physical suffering. I was going to be careless with my body and mind. And I was also going to be ruthless with the emotions of those who cared about me, my parents, my sisters, my friends.

Why this way out?

Like most women I wanted to impress men. Perhaps some men would be impressed by good looks, or a talent for homemaking—cooking and the like. But I was not exceptionally beautiful, not an exceptionally good cook, not an exceptional homemaker. And I think that men are more impressed by things that they think only men can do—climb mountains, cross deserts, penetrate jungles. Or sail the oceans. I wanted to do something which would not only give me intrinsic pleasure but would also impress people and so bring in its wake further opportunities to change my whole way of life.

When I set sail from Milford Haven for America I took along with me the hope that when I had crossed the ocean I would also have crossed the threshold of a new world for myself which would hold the fulfillment of my dreams of fame.

It all started with a voyage the previous year to the Azores. I had given up my job and spent the summer sailing with two men to Spain and the Azores. I thoroughly enjoyed myself and learned a lot about boats—how they behave, how to handle them, how to navigate. When I got back I went to work again, but soon found that I was dreaming of wide seas, blue skies, and the unconstrained life of an ocean sailor. It was only a daydream, but a daydream taken seriously, for as part of the game I made out lists of chandlery, stores and equipment which would be needed for an Atlantic crossing. It was fun reading the lists published by actual voyagers, comparing them with what I thought necessary and seeing where we differed.

But it was only at the International Boat Show in London, at the beginning of January, that I realized how seriously I was considering the crossing. I discovered myself looking at those exciting pieces of gear that hold so much romantic promise for sailing people and wondering which ones I would buy. The dream had overtaken me; the planning had gone too far; I could no longer pull out.

I was like someone whose eye has been caught by a new automobile. It looks really nice, so you think you will find out a bit more about it. You compare it with other cars, and it is so much more desirable. Then you happen to be passing a showroom. Why not go in and have a look? It looks good. And why shouldn't you have one?

You can't get it out of your head. You have just got to have that car. So you buy it.

I bought myself a trans-Atlantic voyage.

Well, why not?

Surely it would be madness even to try? I had never sailed a yacht single-handed. My longest solo passage was about eight miles in a dinghy. On the trip to the Azores the previous year I had seen the power of a gale-torn ocean. But then there were three of us. Could I, alone, hope to survive 4,000 miles of sea and weeks of solitude?

How many women would even consider it? A thousand? Ten? A few had. A woman had crossed the Atlantic alone, a British girl named Ann Davison. But she went the downwind route, stopping on the way in Spain, Morocco, and the Canary Isles. Edith Baumann, a German, had tried the nonstop crossing, but her boat broke up off the Azores and, after taking to a life raft, she and her little dog were picked from the sea. She had escaped with her life. Could I escape with mine?

It was now mid-January. I should not leave Britain later than mid-June if I hoped for reasonable weather. I had to give three months notice to my boss. The decision could not be postponed.

For several days I thought of nothing else. I would sit staring into space, a book unread in my hand. I would go to sleep imagining the difficulties involved and wake with the thoughts still chasing around in my mind.

Still, I could find no good reason for not going. So I decided to go.

## TWO

# *Preparations*

Now THAT I had decided to go, I handed in my resignation from work and got down to planning the project.

The first thing to decide was how much money I could spend. I reckoned that if I cashed all my assets I could afford to buy a boat for about $7,500, pay for the extra gear it might need, and still have a bit left over for contingencies.

What sort of boat should I get? I wanted the longest boat I could handle because the longer a boat is, the faster it will travel. The biggest boat I had sailed in was 25 feet long, and from that experience I thought I would be able to handle one 30 feet long but no more. The boat would have to be secondhand, and not very new at that or it would be too expensive. I looked at the advertisements for boats in the yachting magazines to see what was available, and consulted Peter Pattinson, in whose boat *Pinta of Pembroke* I had sailed the previous year to Spain and the Azores. Between us we decided that a Pionier class boat, a fast cruiser-racer made of fiber-glass, would be most suitable. The design had been well proved in ocean racing where boats are really driven hard, so I knew it would be able to stand up to the hammering it would get from the Atlantic.

I set about trying to find a Pionier in good condition. A strike of postal and telephone workers made it difficult to get in touch with people who were advertising their boats for sale, but I had a slice of luck. A chance visit to the Poole Yacht Centre Company led to an appointment to see a Pionier which was lying at Cowes, on the Isle of Wight.

As I crossed from the mainland to the Isle of Wight on the ferry boat I felt excited and rather nervous. I had never had such a responsibility before, had never bought anything more expensive than a new car. And I was a little nervous about making a fool of myself in front of the owner, asking the wrong questions or not asking the right ones.

When I saw the boat lying moored alongside a motor launch, I was not certain whether I was looking at the right boat. She looked small from the shore, but as I was rowed out by the owner, Ric Carpenter, I could see that she was larger and had elegant, slim lines. The hull was sky blue, and the topsides were white.

I went aboard. She looked to be in good condition. The inside was almost perfect, and she had a set of new curtains, which showed that someone cared for her. As far as I could tell from a brief examination, the hull and rigging were sound, aside from a few surface cracks in the deck. She seemed to have had little use; the plastic windows were transparent with little crazing, which was unusual for a boat eight years old. I liked the look of her and decided to negotiate a price.

After some haggling, Ric Carpenter agreed to sell her to me for £3,350, provided that a professional examination was satisfactory to me. The boat was lifted out of the water and examined, and no serious defects were found. The sale was then completed and I became the proud owner of a yacht named *Aziz*, an Arabic word meaning "magnificent," or "beautiful." The boat had been named after the first owner's favorite polo pony.

*Aziz* was quite a contrast to the only boat I had owned before—an eleven-foot sailing dinghy I had built in the bedroom of my flat in Bristol three years earlier. *Aziz* was 30 feet long, nearly 8 feet wide and weighed about 3½ tons.

She was sloop-rigged, which means she carried two sails at a time, one in front of the mast and one behind. She had two cabins. The roof of the main cabin rose above the level of the decks. Leading from the main cabin, a forward cabin lay under the foredeck and contained two bunks with stowage space underneath.

JOHN BATCHELOR

JOHN BATCHELOR

The main cabin was about ten feet long. It contained two seats, one on each side, a semienclosed lavatory cubicle, a small hanging locker, and a cooking area with a sink and a gas ring. There were a number of lockers for stowing things, and a shelf with cutouts to hold plates and pots. One of the seats in the cabin was large enough for a man to sleep on. The other was only large enough for a child. A quarter berth, which I intended to sleep in, extended aft like a tunnel out of the cabin underneath the starboard cockpit seat. It would be difficult to fall out of, even if the boat turned right over.

*Aziz* had a wardrobe of five headsails, one mainsail, and two spinnakers. The headsails, in order of size, were a genoa, which reached up the forestay to the top of the mast and reached back to the middle of the cabin windows; a small genoa; a No. 1 jib; a No. 2 jib; and a storm jib, which reached about a third of the way up the forestay and stretched only a few feet back. I decided to get a No. 3 jib, as the difference in size between the No. 2 and the storm jib seemed too great.

The mainsail boom was fitted with roller reefing gear for reducing the area of sail presented to the wind. This works rather like a roller blind. You wind a handle and the boom rotates, wrapping the sail around it. The mainsail was also fitted with reefing holes, a row of holes parallel to the boom through which a rope can be taken and the sail tied down on the boom to reduce the area. Three sets of holes ensured that I could tie in one, two, or three reefs, depending on how much less sail area I wanted.

The spinnakers were of no use to me; I had never used one of these brightly colored balloon sails, and didn't intend to learn now. These sails are difficult to handle, even with a full crew, and I thought that I would use twin headsails, one poled out each side, to catch any light winds from astern. Not so efficient, perhaps, but much less likely to cause trouble.

People who have never sailed are often surprised that it is possible to sail into the wind. It is all a question of the way the sails are cut and what angle they make to the wind. When the wind is coming from behind the boat the sails are spread out so that the wind will push the boat, along. When the wind is coming from a direction more or less in front of the boat, the sails act like an aircraft wing, their curve creating "lift," which pulls the boat forward. One can get a boat to head about 45° from the direction the wind is coming from but not much closer. The closer one wants to sail to the wind the more tightly the sails must be pulled.

While arranging the purchase of *Aziz*, I had also been planning the voyage. I decided to leave from Dale, a small village on the fine natural harbor of Milford Haven in southwest Wales, and to aim for Newport, Rhode Island, a well known American yachting center.

I chose Dale for several reasons. I had sailed from there with Peter Pattinson on the Azores trip and knew that I would be able to get all the help I needed there. I would not be ignored when I wanted something as I might be in a larger port. By departing from Dale I would avoid having to sail down the English Channel, with its constant heavy shipping. I would be a hundred miles north of the Channel, which would give me an advantage when sailing into the prevailing westerly winds of the Atlantic.

At first I had thought of heading for New York, the place many British people think of as the capital of America. But when I thought of the problems of entering an unknown and busy port, I quickly changed my mind. I would not know where to tie up, and I could see myself getting in the way of the big ships. I looked at the chart of the North Atlantic and decided that Newport would be the best place to arrive. Since it is south of Cape Cod, I wouldn't have to negotiate the difficult waters of the Gulf of Maine.

As a compromise between leaving early enough to reduce the chance of encountering a hurricane on the other side of the ocean and leaving me enough time to get ready, I settled on Saturday, June 12, as my departure date. This would be six weeks after finishing my job in Cardiff, and I determined that by the time I left Cardiff I would have prepared detailed lists of everything I would need so that I would not be rushing madly around at the last minute.

On Friday, April 9, I went to Cowes to pick up *Aziz*. The following day Ric, his friend Sue, and I set off down the Channel on the first stage of the passage around Land's End to Dale. I was glad that Ric could come, for he would be able to show me the ropes. I had never been responsible for a yacht. Suddenly *Aziz* looked huge, the sails seemed vast, and the mast seemed to touch the clouds.

There was a strong breeze that day and we reached Weymouth quickly, tying alongside a large yacht for the night. Next morning we rounded Portland Bill with very little wind, crossed Lyme Bay, and arrived in Torquay, where I reluctantly left *Aziz*.

I was pleased with the way *Aziz* handled on this passage. She seemed responsive to the helm, quite fast, and—most important—the sails seemed fairly easy to manage. I had been worried that I would find it exhausting raising and lowering them, but it was not such hard work after all.

There was one disappointment en route. The self-steering gear that I had had fitted at Cowes did not work and showed no sign of ever working. The principle of self-steering gear is to use the power of the wind to turn the rudder when the boat is off course. The simplest system is to have a vane linked to the main rudder in such a way that when the boat changes its heading with respect to the wind, the vane turns, activates the rudder, and brings the boat back on the original heading. Such a system only works with a very large vane area. It is more usual to have either an auxiliary rudder much smaller than the main one, or to use a servo blade that harnesses the power of the water, using it to turn the main rudder.

The system I had fitted at Cowes had the vane directly linked to the rudder but did not have the power to turn it. I got in touch with another Pionier owner who had the same gear and he said that his had never worked properly. As I did not have time to fiddle around I decided to cut my losses and get one which was sure to work, so I ordered a Hasler-Gibbs servo pendulum system, the type used by Francis Chichester in *Gypsy Moth IV*, Alec Rose in *Lively Lady*, and Chay Blyth in *British Steel*. Luckily there was one in stock which was promptly delivered to Torquay. There was no time to fit it there, so I stowed the parts away in the forecabin to be taken around to Dale.

I left *Aziz* in Torquay for three weeks until I had finished my job in Cardiff. Each weekend I went down and lived aboard, getting used to the gear and doing little jobs such as checking the electric circuits. With each visit I became more at ease, as one does in a new house. I was able to move around the deck without tripping over things, and could lay my hands on what I wanted without difficulty. *Aziz* stopped being a stranger and became a friend.

On May 1, I sailed out of Torquay with a friend and headed for the Scilly Isles. These low but rocky islands mark the western end of the Channel. I planned to stay there for a few days before heading north for Wales. We had a very quiet passage and motored most of the way from the Lizard, the southern peninsula of Cornwall. About four miles from the islands we ran out of gas. One gallon on the tank dipstick, I discovered, meant no fuel for the engine.

We hoisted the biggest sails to catch the tiny breeze

and crept toward the hazy shore of St. Mary's. As the evening wore on we eased up St. Mary's Sound and approached the harbor. The wind died. Out came the dinghy oars. We laboriously paddled over the stern and crept round the rocks. A fishing launch came alongside and offered us a tow, and thus ingloriously we entered the harbor. We anchored, tidied up, and then rowed ashore for a well-earned drink in the Mermaid bar.

Despite the anticlimax of being towed into port, I was pleased with the trip. We had arrived in the right place, so my navigation had passed. *Aziz* had shown that she would keep moving even in the lightest wind, which cheered me when I thought of the calm weather I could expect around the Azores.

The weather soon changed. I spent six days in the islands being blasted by strong winds. When I left for Dale, a fresh south-southeast wind pushed the boat along but also made her roll hideously since both wind and sea were coming from behind. Both of my crew on this passage were very seasick; luckily I was not. I did most of the steering during the day, but insisted on having some time off watch in the night. Fatigue can play hell with judgment, and I did not want to approach land without having slept.

We lurched over the sea at a good speed and sighted land at dawn, before it was obscured by heavy rain. It was a bedraggled crew which finally dropped the anchor off Dale, and rowed hurriedly ashore. I had enjoyed the trip and had seen *Aziz* behave well in fresh winds. I think the crew wished they were dead.

From then on I lived on *Aziz* and worked full-time on preparing her for the crossing. The major work to be done was the fitting of the Hasler self-steering gear and the making of board covers to strengthen the windows, which were 6 feet long and vulnerable to breaking seas. Although I did a lot of small jobs, these two major ones were done by Brian Henshall of the Dale Sailing Company. Brian is an excellent craftsman, but he will not be hurried. I spent a lot of time biting my fingernails until I discovered that in Pembrokeshire things always get done in the end, and get done well. It is just that there is no show of urgency.

I enjoyed my weeks in Dale. I was looked after very well by Campbell Reynolds, the owner of the Dale Sailing Company, and his wife, Mil, who fed me vast quantities of food and tea and made me feel really at home. Bill Tamsett, the proprietor of the Griffin Inn, was helpful and cheerful, taking telephone messages for me and fending off unwanted callers. Mr. and Mrs. Rind allowed me the use of their deliciously large bathtub, which is a world apart. Bunty Cowan, the Secretary of the Dale Yacht Club, was very helpful, even to the extent of washing some decidedly nasty sailing clothes. And everyone was ready for a friendly talk.

I planned to sail single-handed to Ireland at the Spring Bank Holiday to try out the self-steering gear, and myself. Peter Pattinson, in *Pinta*, and John Redfern, in his boat *Sloop John D*, planned to make the crossing as well, so I anticipated a good weekend.

*Preparations*

On the Friday I was due to leave, *Aziz* was ashore on the trolley, and Brian and I worked furiously to finish fitting the self-steering gear in time to catch the evening tide. We made it with about forty minutes to spare, and *Aziz* was launched at about 1930 hours. I motored to a buoy and spent the next hour tidying up and preparing to leave, while Brian spliced an eye into a new anchor rope. At 2130 hours Brian rowed off in his dinghy. I hoisted the sails, dropped the mooring, and set off on my first single-handed passage.

As soon as I was clear of the moored boats, I latched in the self-steering gear and let go of the tiller. Would it work? I watched the boat's wake, and to my great delight found that it steered straighter than I did. I had a good helmsman aboard with me.

There was a stout wind, and we creamed along through the darkness, well heeled over. As I tacked past Skokholm Island, I caught the edge of the Wild Goose Race, and we crashed into great holes in the sea, sheets of phosphorescent spray flying from the bows. The tide carried me well north, and as the night wore on the wind dropped to a gentle breeze.

I went on to the foredeck to change to a bigger foresail. It was the first time I had changed sail alone at night, and because I was tired the motion of the foredeck made me feel a bit queasy. It was an effort to haul up the sail, and when I had finished I just lay back on the sail bag on the foredeck and went to sleep for a few minutes. Eventually I recovered enough to go back to the cockpit.

I spent an anxious hour wondering whether I was getting too close to the South Bishop lighthouse. I finally convinced myself that all was well and turned in for a couple of hours sleep. When I awoke at dawn I could see some islands to the east, from which I could work out my position.

The wind rose during the morning, and soon *Aziz* was going pretty fast, the wind behind her. The self-steering gear seemed able to cope, although the boat was yawing from side to side a bit. In the middle of the morning I sighted a sail ahead. It appeared to be going the same way, and gradually I overhauled it, guessing that it would be *Pinta*. It was, and I was encouraged to think that my navigation was sound. I overtook *Pinta* at noon as we both rounded the Conningbeg lightship, and arrived in Dunmore East at about 1630 hours. I tacked into the harbor to lie alongside *Sloop John D. Pinta* arrived about three-quarters of an hour later and tied alongside *Aziz*. We all went to the yacht club and had a drink and discussed the crossing.

I had arrived in the right place, at a reasonable speed, and nothing disastrous had happened. The self-steering gear had worked well. I had not worked badly. I had managed the sail changes without enormous difficulty, although I had found it rather exhausting, probably because I was feeling mildly seasick. I felt more confident that I could sail *Aziz* single-handed.

The crews of all three boats ganged up for a splendid seafood meal at the Ocean Hotel. We dressed up for the occasion to prove that one can remain civilized even when living in cramped quarters and had a convivial evening. The next day was spent idling about the village checking the quality of the local brew. In the evening we went out for another good meal and some dancing at a discothèque before rolling back to our respective boats. We changed clothes, hoisted the sails, and cast off for the return to Wales.

There was hardly a breath of wind. After a while, we all started our engines, and *Pinta* and *Sloop John D* were soon out of sight in the darkness. I motored for about an hour so as to get an offing. Then I switched off. I never got the engine running again, so had a very slow passage back. I drifted up and down on the tides and took twenty-four hours to cover the last eighteen miles. As in the Scillies, I was towed in the final few hundred yards.

I was now sure that I could handle the boat. I had ten days left to get everything done. Brian started work on the windows, making some splendid boards with small plastic portlights cut in them. I started the final collection of stores and equipment. Life became very hectic. One delightful but counterproductive influence was the parties which were given for me. Dale Yacht Club gave me a good do at Sunday lunchtime with the result that I went aboard *Aziz* and spilled a pot of paint over the cockpit floor.

Time rushed by and before I knew what had happened there were only two days left until Saturday, June 12, departure day.

# THREE

# Leaving

ONLY TWO days left. Things really started moving. I had allowed time to get all the stores on board and stored away on Thursday, before going to Milford Haven dock on the evening tide so that I could complete customs formalities on Friday.

I had unfortunately not allowed time for talking to the press and broadcasting men. And dozens seemed to turn up, all wanting interviews, all certain that they only needed a couple of minutes, all taking as long as they could get.

Brian was still working on *Aziz*, fitting wood battens to the after bulkhead and to the washboards for closing the cabin entrance to strengthen them. I spent the morning getting the food aboard with the assistance of press-ganged newsmen. Frankly I cannot remember exactly what happened that day. I know that I did two television interviews on board, which took up a lot of time. I know that I did some television interviews ashore, for I remember using an anchor as a "prop" and being delighted to discover that it was one I had ordered but had given up for lost.

Peter Pattinson arrived before lunch bringing a number of plastic water containers for me. Shortly afterward came Shirley Marsham, who had sailed with me to the Scilly Isles the previous year as crew in Peter's boat. She brought me a splendid selection of Tupperware containers, a present from the makers. These airtight plastic containers make it much easier to keep food dry and tidy.

My parents arrived with Phyllida, my second sister, who had had her leave from her Foreign Office post in the Arabian Gulf put ahead so that she could see me off. We had time for a short talk before I was whisked off to do some job. I was sorry not to have more time with them, but I arranged to see them in Milford the next day.

I finally escaped from the fuss ashore and went aboard to get ready to take *Aziz* up to Milford. Peter came aboard, and Brian decided to continue working while we moved up the haven. We motored past the oil jetties and dredgers and arrived outside the dock gates just as they were opening, a beautiful piece of timing. A lovely white ketch came out very quickly and shot off up the haven. We cautiously approached the gates, decided that nothing else was coming out, and motored slowly in.

I managed to bring *Aziz* alongside a docked lighter without hitting it a terrible thump, despite my ham-fisted use of the engine controls. We tied up and climbed over the rubber tires surrounding the lighter and found that we were only a few minutes' walk from the road entrance. A much better place to be than the corner where yachts usually go, an interminable walk around the fish dock from the entrance.

We spent a few minutes tidying up, and then Peter and I walked up to the Lord Nelson Hotel where he was to stay. I had a bath and changed into shore clothes, and after a drink we had a good dinner. Then I walked back to *Aziz*, cleared the junk off my berth, and went into a sound sleep.

I woke at about 7:30 and walked up to the hotel for the last civilized breakfast I was to have for many a day.

Now the enormity of the whole project hit me. What the hell was I doing? I was going to be alone for an immense time. I might die. I might never see my friends again. I had been so happy the past few weeks doing the things I liked and living among friendly and interesting people. These weeks had been among the happiest of my life, and now I had to give them up, to start a new phase of life, to face the unknown. I didn't want to.

But I was committed to the project, so I stiffened my upper lip and got on with it. With the return to work came the return of confidence and enthusiasm.

## Leaving

When I returned to *Aziz*, I was discovered by a photographer who wanted some stills for the BBC. Then Peter came to say that we could tie alongside a tug exactly opposite the dock entrance. This would be much more convenient for loading stores, so we motored around.

I went up to the customshouse and obtained my clearance papers quickly. Then I went to see the Waterguard, who are responsible for the loading and sealing of duty-free stores. As they did not yet have loading time, I went back to work on *Aziz*.

My parents and Phyllida arrived and produced cans and bags of homemade cakes and cookies. I had specially requested some of my mother's homemade fruit cake and parkin, a North Country cake made with oatmeal and treacle. The family came aboard and looked at the shambles in the cabin while I wrote a list of the fresh fruit and vegetables I wanted and various other things I had forgotten to get—such as pencil and paper for writing a diary. If I had forgotten those, this book would not have been written.

The family went shopping, and Peter and I started to stow the stores, which were lying higgledy-piggledy on the forward berths. This took quite a while, decanting the dry foods into Tupperware and packing the cans in the small well with the canvas boom cover, which I would not need at sea, so that the cans would not rattle around. It turned out to be an unwise move to use the cover, for the cans eventually rusted and stained the canvas.

The rest of the food went on the berths in the for-

33

ward cabin, much of it in Tupperware and the rest in cardboard boxes or loose. I jammed it tightly together and tied a length of lobster pot netting over it to hold everything in place. Also in the forward cabin went ten gallons of water in clear plastic containers, eight gallons of kerosene in yellow plastic containers, the large anchor, spare oilskins, camera box, spare battens, spare tiller, anchor buoy, a few books and a roll of charts which should have been left behind as they were for the English Channel.

I was worried that all this weight at the front would make *Aziz* nose-heavy, for I had only ten gallons of gasoline in the after locker to compensate. However, she seemed all right, and I consoled myself with the thought that all my stores would weigh less than a couple of hefty foredeck hands sleeping in the forward berths.

By lunchtime a dour rain was pouring from a uniformly gray sky. The family arrived laden with bags of stores and with food for a picnic lunch, and we all crammed into the cabin among the jumble of stores, chandlery, and tools. Of course, this had to be the time that the Waterguard came to seal up the bonded stores. It was so wet outside that everyone squeezed into the cabin like sardines in a tin. The bonded stores were checked and the paperwork completed. The spirits and cigarettes were sealed in the locker under the galley, which I had rapidly transformed into a bond locker by screwing an eye on to the frame so that string could be taken from the door handle to the eye and sealed with the official lead seal.

## Leaving

My parents did more shopping during the afternoon while Peter, Brian, and I carried on working aboard. Brian was working on deck, rigging extra life lines and strengthening the bracket for the self-steering gear. Peter and I tidied up the cabin using my usual technique of putting everything into lockers and boxes and arranging the boxes neatly on the floor. Peter's boy, Robert, arrived and changed into sailing clothes, and soon we were ready to leave the Milford dock to return to Dale.

We motored out of the dock when the gates opened and headed down the haven with rain still pouring from a gray overcast. We were chased by a motor boat with photographers aboard, so we raised the sails to make a more impressive picture. There was a good breeze accompanying the rain, and we went very fast and soon got back to Dale. The wind made it difficult to row to the beach, about half a mile from the mooring, so Peter put me ashore at the nearest point. I climbed up the hill to the road and walked down to the village. I savored the few minutes by myself after the pressures of the day, but I could not dawdle as Phyllida was waiting for me in Dale.

While Phyllida drove me to Haverfordwest, I changed from jeans and oilskins to a dress, and looked quite respectable when we arrived at Chez Gilbert, the best restaurant in the area. The family group had expanded to include my third sister, Primrose, and my Uncle Jack and his wife. Unfortunately my eldest sister, Gillian, could not come. We had a good meal—my last meal ashore—but I was really too tired to appreciate it. I hurried back to Dale and rowed out to Peter's boat where I was to sleep, Peter being moored much closer to the beach than *Aziz*. I fell quickly into a dreamless sleep.

The next morning I awoke to the realization that the great day had arrived. I was worried that I would not be ready to leave at 1100 hours, my announced departure time. Peter and I fetched *Aziz* from her mooring and anchored her by *Pinta* so that she was as close to shore as possible. I would have to leave on time now, or the falling tide would leave the boat aground. Brian turned up in his dinghy and got to work on some final jobs that he thought needed doing. I rowed ashore to meet the family and to see Bruce Coward, my literary agent, who had brought the contract for this book to be signed. This was important, for the nonreturnable advance to be paid would almost cover the costs of the trip, apart from the boat, which was insured. Even if I were forced to give up, I would not be in debt.

By the time I had been through the contract, clause by clause, and signed each page, quite a crowd had gathered. I was delighted to see my friends Jock and Doreen Ferguson, who had been among the first to know of my trans-Atlantic plans, and had driven all the way from Bristol that morning. After kisses all around, with my tears held back, I left the beach and rowed back to *Aziz*. I was not to set foot on British soil until two months had passed.

As eleven o'clock approached, the water became more and more crowded with boats of all shapes and sizes from rowing dinghies to Campbell's converted lifeboat. They sailed around and around *Aziz*, and I felt like the statue of Eros in the center of Piccadilly Circus. One launch got too close and fouled my anchor warp but fortunately did not unhook us from the bottom. I was getting impatient to go, but Brian insisted that we fit the plastic pipes to the spare bilge pump. This involved boiling a kettle of water to soften the pipes. It seemed to take ages to boil, but eventually it got hot enough and Brian squeezed the pipes onto the pump.

I hurried him into his dinghy, asked Peter and Robert to hoist the sails, and at 1115 hours the anchor was hauled up and we were off.

Peter and Robert stayed aboard to fend off any overfriendly boats. I took the tiller and swung *Aziz* round to head out past Dale Fort to the open sea. There was a stiff breeze from the northwest, and I had quite a job trying to sail single-handed without the self-steering latched in, as my hands were full of ropes. I had hardly a moment to watch the escort of boats that followed me, weaving to and fro across my wake. The launch carrying a television crew tried to interview me by loudspeaker, but I could not understand what was said, besides having *Aziz* and the other boats to attend to. I waved to my family and friends, but I was really longing to be alone, away from the tensions of the last few days.

As we approached St. Ann's Head and the ocean, I could see that there was a big swell coming in. I brought *Aziz* head to wind and held her there while Peter and Robert climbed into their rubber dinghy, a perilous operation as the craft bobbed up and down on the swell.

I cast off their painter and left them astern to be picked up by the television launch. Then I set the self-steering gear and streamed the log to mark the start of the crossing.

Now I had nothing to do but watch the fleet. One by one they turned back to the shelter of the haven until eventually just *Aziz* and a white yacht were heading out to sea. Finally she too turned back with a parting wave from her crew.

At last I was alone.

*Aziz* (above) about to be launched for the trip to Ireland. Right, Nicki and stores a few days before leaving.

Left, the last morning before the transatlantic crossing—preparing to leave. *(Photo Mary Nilnes Walker)*

Leaving the beach for the last time.

*Aziz* under way—streaming the log line. *(Photo Peter Patinson)*

Left, view from the stern to the main cabin. Right, the galley.

Left, the shambles below. Right, the navigation area and the opening to the quarter berth.

Right, taking a sextant sight.
Below, evening in a calm.

Above, self-portrait at sea.
Left, the Hasler Gibbs
self-steering gear.

Sunset mid-Atlantic.

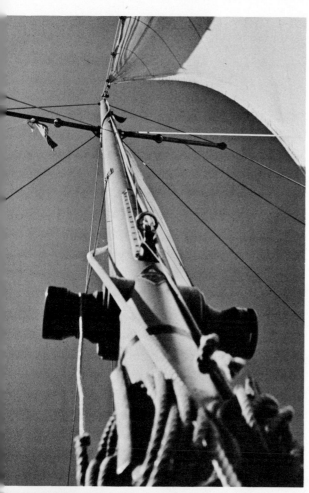

Left, the view up the mast. Below, weed wrapped around the log line.

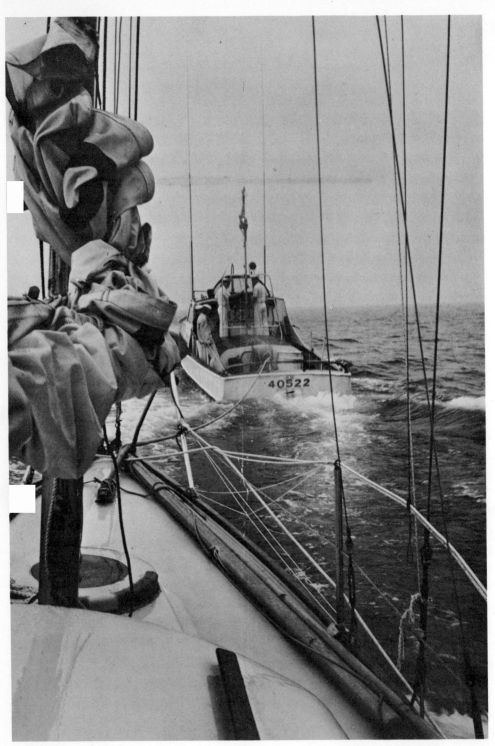

Journey's end—following U.S. Coast Guard to
Newport, Rhode Island.

*FOUR*

# First Gale

I wasn't alone after all.

A light aircraft sped over the wave tops and passed immediately above me. I waved. It circled and came over again and continued to make passes over the boat. I guessed that it was taking photographs of me and was rather flattered by such attention, but I soon got bored with waving and wished that he would go away so that I could be sick in private. I went below, and soon he went away. I know now that he was supposed to film my departure with all the boats for television, and that he was heartily cursed for being late.

47

The weather improved steadily, and the sun came out. *Aziz* was going well, but I felt queasy and was actually sick several times. I wasn't surprised at this as I am always sick the first day at sea, but after that I never have any trouble, even in the most turbulent seas. However, it is unpleasant at the time, and I didn't feel like working. I spent some time in my berth and some time in the cockpit, smoking. I have always found that smoking helps me feel less sick although I know that many people do not feel that way. A friend has told me that vile cigars are the thing, but I only had mild cigarettes. Maybe I should have taken tobacco twist to chew like the sailors of old. One trouble about feeling sick when sailing alone is that you dare not take a powerful tablet such as Dramamine, as it is so soporific. You have to stick it out.

Apart from the sickness, I thought I was feeling quite happy, and wrote in my diary, "I am feeling remarkably calm after this morning when I had a little cry and wished I wasn't going." But when I recorded on tape an account of the departure, I was quite overcome by emotion. The tape is full of long pauses and choked sentences. I wanted to go back and tell everyone what a marvelous send-off it had been. I wanted to share my emotions with someone else.

I felt guilty about letting my parents in for an unpleasant few weeks. They had not let me know their true feelings, not wanting to influence my decision, but I knew that they would worry, for what parents wouldn't? I was much better off than my family and friends—I would always know how I was whereas they would be left to imagine all sorts of ghastly things. They would have no news of me unless I was able to talk to a passing ship. Apart from a short-range distress radio I was not carrying a radio transmitter. If I did die, no one would know how or when it happened.

This was my worst fear for those ashore: that I would just not reappear and that eventually they would have to give up hope. Not that I thought I would die. I would not have embarked on such a venture unless I thought that the chance of surviving was very good.

As far as I could see, there were two possible occurrences which might kill me. One was falling overboard. I frequently had a vision of being in the water watching *Aziz* sailing beautifully over the horizon, the self-steering gear dutifully holding her on course for America. If a boat steered by hand is left unattended, she will gradually swing round until the sails are flapping and she stops making way through the water, and there is a chance of getting aboard. But under self-steering, the boat just carries on. However, as I can hardly swim, I thought that going overboard would be my funeral in either case. I determined to wear a harness with a line that I could clip to the boat for all deck work.

The other possible disaster was being run down by a ship. All vessels are supposed to carry navigation lights and to keep a continuous lookout. I could not carry efficient navigation lights since these require a lot of energy to be visible at a useful range. I could not use electric power as it would have meant running the engine daily, and I could not carry enough fuel for that. I could not use oil lamps because again, I could not carry enough fuel.

What I intended doing was displaying a single white light instead of the red and green navigation lights. This light was to come from a Tilley lamp, a gadget which burns vaporized kerosene. It has a tank of kerosene, which is vaporized by preheating a jet with burning methyl alcohol and pumping air into the tank to crate pressure. The vapor burns round a filament, like a gas light, and gives an intense white light.

I could not hope to keep an effective lookout in these days of high-speed ships when a ship can be below the horizon only a quarter of an hour before it passes by you—or over you. I decided that I would keep some sort of a lookout when I was in the shipping lanes but otherwise would not bother. After all, the Atlantic is a big place, and a ship has to pass within feet to be dangerous, except in heavy weather when a ship's wake can combine with big seas to swamp or capsize a small boat.

I had one safety device: a radar reflector. This is made from three intersecting mutually perpendicular sheets of aluminum, and is designed to reflect radar beams and give a bright spot on a ship's radar scope—if anyone cares to look. I hardly dare complain about poor lookouts, but I believe that many merchant ships do not keep any sort of a watch at sea. Judging by the number of collisions and near misses in the English Channel, many ships do not keep an effective watch there. And that is the busiest stretch of water in the world. Why should they bother in mid-ocean?

Apart from these hazards I could not foresee anything to stop me from surviving. Even if I were dismasted or the rudder fell off or some other such thing happened, I could call for help on my distress radio. I had an inflatable liferaft, which was kept in the cockpit ready for immediate use, and I had flares and smoke flares close at hand.

I would, of course, be reluctant to ask for help, but would do so if it were obviously the only sensible thing to do. People are very good about helping yachtsmen in distress, regardless of inconvenience, but when one undertakes a hazardous voyage one should not rely on help. One must be prepared to live and die unaided and not impose on the goodwill of others.

Whether I would be able to complete the crossing without disturbing my personality was another question. The thought of forty days alone did not appall me, for I had my books and radio, but I was not sure how I would react to being frightened. I did not know whether I would be able to stand frequent frightening circumstances, but was encouraged by the knowledge that a fair number of men have done this or longer crossings without ending up completely insane. Nevertheless, I was a bit worried by the story of Donald Crowhurst, who, I had been told, went mad at sea and committed suicide. I couldn't visualize myself doing that, but how could I tell what six weeks without companionship would do to me? I tried not to think about it.

It was my first night at sea. The sun sank like a red glob into the water, and darkness soon came. As I had seen a lot of ships and fishing boats during the day, I lit the Tilley lamp and hung it on the boom. It gave a brilliant light, completely ruining my night vision so that I had to shade my eyes from the light when looking for other ships' lights. To my annoyance, the lamp spluttered and died after about an hour, so I pumped it and relit it before going below for an hour's sleep. When I came out again, I could see the lights of two fishing vessels quite close. Both altered course to pass astern, so I felt that the light was doing its job. But shortly afterward, I saw the lights of a big ship heading for me. She did not alter course, and I had to unlatch the self-steering and change course to pass astern of her. I was sure that she had not seen me, which was rather worrying.

I slept in short spells because the lamp kept going out. I couldn't find out why and was depressed at the thought of having to tend it continuously. Later I discovered that it was necessary to fill the tank as full as possible and pump it a lot to get good pressure in the tank. It was still necessary to flick the on-off knob occasionally to clear the carbon deposit which formed in the jet.

It started raining at 0400 hours and kept at it until 1000 hours. Fortunately the wind was from abeam and not astern, so the rain did not pour in through the companionway, and I did not have to put the washboards in. I hate being in the cabin with the exit closed—I feel cut off from the boat and the weather.

By 0700 hours the wind had increased a bit and I changed from the No. 1 jib to the No. 2 jib. This was wet work: green water was pouring over me as the bows dipped into the waves. Nevertheless, I enjoyed it. My new oilskins turned out to be very waterproof, even around the neck where there is usually a leak.

During the morning the wind started to drop, and by afternoon I had the maximum sail area raised, full main and big genoa. I spent the day nibbling food, listening to the radio, and reorganizing the chaos. I felt lonely, as I wanted to tell someone about the trials of the night and the previous day's send-off. To my delight I found a bag with unopened telegrams in it, so I had fun opening them and finding out who had remembered me.

By evening there was very little wind, and the sea was smooth. I had noticed that the radar reflector, which was mounted between the starboard lower shrouds, was chafing the mainsail. I decided that as *Aziz* was not rolling much I would haul myself up the mast to the crosstrees and wrap the reflector in rags (so called, really a rather nice tea towel with a green giraffe on it). This was my first experience in going up the mast at sea. I had a block-and-tackle system specially made for this. The top block was hoisted to the top of the mast on a spare halyard. A line attached to this block ran around a ratchet block attached to me, up over the masthead block and down to my hands, so that I had a considerable mechanical advantage and could lift my own weight. The lower block was attached to a canvas bosun's chair, once described to me as a "bottom bra," which I sat in. I could cleat the downhaul line to hold myself in any position and free both hands.

I was able to haul myself up easily but rather slowly.

As I hadn't dropped the mainsail, I couldn't twine my legs around the mast and swung about as *Aziz* rolled. I scraped some skin off the inside of my thighs trying to grip the mast with them. I tied the tea towel around the reflector, but it was obviously not a good solution; it would be sure to come adrift sooner or later. Still, it was better than nothing. Later I would have to think of something better.

After these exertions on deck I went below and amused myself for an hour by making a code flag. Each letter of the alphabet is represented by a different flag so that one can communicate between ships. They also each have a special meaning. I was carrying the following flags:

O—the yellow flag which must be flown on entering a foreign port.

K—"I wish to communicate with you."

V—"I require assistance."

U—"You are running into danger."

*Aziz* has a four-letter code MSOT, which could be flown to identify her. I hadn't been able to get hold of a T-flag and so had to make one.

Fortunately, the T-flag is not very complicated as it is a tricolor of red, white, and blue. I made it out of a maroon shirt tail, a white petticoat, and a blue chiffon scarf. It was, I hoped, recognizable if not beautiful. I rewarded myself with a supper of shrimp cocktail, cucumber, tomato, and raw carrot. Soon I went to bed.

The wind increased in strength throughout the night, and with it the waves rose. At 0300 hours I was awakened by the sound of pouring rain and got up to change from genoa to the No. 1 jib. I went back to sleep. When I awoke at 0615 hours, *Aziz* was heeled over and slamming her bows on to the waves. I changed to the No. 2 jib and rolled the mainsail to the first batten, which is about halfway between the first and second sets of reefing holes. At 0900 hours I took off the jib and put another roll in the main, and at 1230 hours I rolled the main right up to the second batten, equivalent to just over three reefs. With all this deckwork, I seemed to spend the whole morning climbing in and out of my oil-skins—I didn't want to keep them on all the time as they were wet outside and would have made a mess in the cabin.

The wind was from just east of north, and I reckoned that it had reached gale force. The seas were about twelve feet high, the gray of Atlantic warships, with white crests and spume dragging down the backs of the waves. They seemed rather confused, probably because I was over the banks which run up the Irish Sea approaches. *Aziz* was sailing fast on a broad reach with the self-steering just managing to hold her on course. I was frightened, for this was the first gale I had been in alone —as well as the first gale I had been in with *Aziz*. I was not sure how each of us would behave and was worried that I was carrying too much sail and straining the boat.

I couldn't decide whether I should allow *Aziz* to continue her headlong rush or should heave to and let her ride the waves gently. I decided to leave her to carry on, mainly because I didn't want to go out on deck to hoist the storm jib. It was cold and wet outside, with water all over the decks, and I didn't want to fight with ropes and sails. I spent most of the day in my bunk waiting for the nasty weather to go away.

I had to go out in the end as one of the lines from the self-steering to the tiller chafed through. I raised the storm jib, hauled it to windward, pulled the mainsail fairly far in, and lashed the tiller about centrally. What happened now was that the jib, being pulled across to the wrong side, was tending to turn the boat away from the wind while the mainsail was trying to turn the boat into the wind. The result was that she lay quietly at about 45° to the wind, slowing moving forward and drifting sideways. It is remarkable how heaving-to changes the noise and lurching of a headlong rush to the peace of a cork bobbing up and down.

I slept fairly well that night, although I woke frequently to the wind whistling through the rigging wires. At 0700 hours the whistling had disappeared, and I decided that I should start sailing again. I renewed the tiller line, unreefed the main to the first batten, and hoisted the No. 2 jib. Then I went below to get some breakfast.

I had just wriggled out of the oilskin jacket and was stripping the trousers off when I heard the jib flogging and cracking. I looked out to see what was wrong and found that the sheet had come adrift from the corner of the jib. I hastily dressed again and went to clip it back on. I didn't want to lower the sail, so I grabbed the flapping corner with one hand and the snap shackle on the sheet in the other hand and tried to clip them together. It was difficult holding on to the floggy canvas without being pulled off balance, although I was leaning against the shrouds with my arms around them, and several times the sail tore itself from my grasp. I was just about to let go the halyard and drop the sail enough to take the wind out of it when I managed to get the clip on.

For breakfast I fried some tomatoes and bread and thoroughly enjoyed them. I was glad that I felt hungry, for I had been worried about my appetite, and I was afraid that I would have to force myself to eat.

I wrote in my diary: "Yesterday has shown me that my reaction to fear is a bad one—I just try to sleep and pretend everything is O.K. Must make myself do things." However, I was more confident now that the gale had blown itself out without anything serious happening. The tiller line had chafed through because it was leading around a sharp edge of the self-steering bracket, so I put another block to keep it clear and give a fair lead.

During the morning I got to work. I started by cutting off the ends of the stainless bolts that Brian had put through the cabin roof and after bulkhead. First I used the little hacksaw but made slow progress, so I tried the large hacksaw but couldn't get at the bolts with that. I finally got out my magnificent boltcroppers, a tool rather like an oversized pair of pliers with handles about three feet long. They were heavy, and, like an idiot, I dropped them on the steering compass, which was mounted on the bulkhead.

Fortunately the glass compass top is a hemisphere

and therefore very strong, and I only chipped a small hole in it. The liquid in the compass started to run out, so I hurriedly got out some flexible sealer and bunged up the hole. It stopped the leak, but there was now a large air bubble in the liquid. I decided that it would be all right—I could still read the figures, and the sealer was on the side away from the steering position and didn't spoil my view of the compass card. I was very annoyed at myself for being so careless.

Then I did another stupid thing. I had two buckets, one a big farming bucket with a metal handle that I had "borrowed" from Peter Pattinson, the other a small domestic bucket with a plastic handle. I had a piece of string tied to the handle of the little bucket so that I could throw it over the side and haul in sea water. I threw it over. The sea caught it with a terrific tug, and the handle came off. My nice little red bucket floated away astern while I was left holding a piece of string with a handle tied on to it—a ridiculous feeling. The most maddening thing was that I knew perfectly well that the handle might come off; it had happened before.

At lunchtime I emptied one of the small plastic water bottles I inherited with *Aziz*. I didn't want it cluttering up the boat, so I decided to throw it overboard. Then I thought I would send a message in it. But it was no good putting a piece of paper inside; no one would notice it. I really wanted to paint on the outside but I didn't have a suitable brush, so I made do with a chinagraph pencil which gives a waxy mark. I wrote my name, the boat's name, the date, my course, and my log reading, and addressed it to Peter Pattinson. It should have drifted up the Channel or the Irish Sea. It has not been reported, but I didn't expect it to be. I just liked the idea of sending a message in a bottle.

The wind continued moderating, and by the afternoon I had the full main and No. 1 jib up. I managed to get a decent noon sight, which put me 250 miles from Dale, not bad going. After my efforts of the morning, I took the afternoon off and idled about reading *The Nun's Story* and puttering around.

My appetite was improving, and when I came across a packet labeled in my mother's writing, "Honey Cake. Eat first," I obeyed the instruction immediately and ate it all along with a cup of China tea with a slice of lemon in it. By evening I was hungry again and made myself a large macaroni Bolognese. I ate it all too, and promptly felt immensely sleepy.

# FIVE

# *Snags*

THE WEATHER was peaceful that night. I had nothing to do except pump up the Tilley lamp periodically. I slept well, apart from these excursions, and finally woke at about 0800 hours. Half an hour later a line of black clouds passed over, bringing a short burst of wind that sent *Aziz* scuttling over the sea. It was soon over, and we continued to potter quietly onward.

I felt pretty rotten though, as if I had a hangover. This wasn't very likely as, for once in my life, I hadn't had a drink for days. Perhaps it was a reaction to sobriety; my body adapting itself to running on pure blood instead of the usual blood-alcohol mix!

## Snags

It felt like flu. I took a couple of aspirin and huddled up in my sleeping bag feeling sorry for myself. I felt miserable all day and kept taking aspirin and then going back to sleep for awhile. During the afternoon, I started to ache all over, and this convinced me that I really did have flu and was not imagining things.

The night was decidedly unpleasant. I kept waking in a sweat and throwing back the sleeping bag to cool off. Then I would get cold and, huddling up again, would go back to sleep, to dream furiously before waking again in a sweat. Fortunately we were all but becalmed throughout the night, so there was no need for me to work the ship at all apart from checking the telltale compass above my head to see that we were on course. Actually this involved more mental effort than you might think. Because the compass was mounted close to various metal instruments, the reading was about 30° in error, so I had to work out what the course really was. Sometimes I would do my calculations wrong and scramble out of bed into the cockpit to look at the steering compass only to find that we were on course after all. If the opposite happened—if I thought *Aziz* was on course when really she was heading in the wrong direction—I never discovered it. But I expect it did happen.

I did nothing to help the boat that night, for it did not seem necessary. Indeed, I doubt whether I could have forced my body out on deck and made it work unless there had been a real panic when I would probably have forgotten about feeling ill. I find that when I am ill my mind and body become more differentiated. Usually I am not aware of being a mind-body union.

Even when there is a difference of opinion between the parts, such as when I have a blister but want to walk, it is the union which decides. However, when ill or drunk or under stress, the union breaks down, and the constituents hold public discussion and decide the issue by a trial of strength.

The character of the whole is determined by the balance struck between the parts. When conditions change so that different stresses are imposed the balance is altered and the character is changed. This was one of the things I was trying to find out about myself: when conditions were seriously threatening the physical part, how would the whole react? Would there be disintegration of the union and, if so, how would the mental part compensate? Would it be able to accept reality, or would it retreat into a world of dreams where the body could no longer overload the mind with unacceptable messages?

One of the possible stresses was illness. When planning the voyage I tried to find out what medical emergencies might arise. It seemed to me that one could divide the possible sources of illness into two types.

The first type would be due to infection, probably by bacteria or viruses already present in or on the body. Such illnesses as bronchitis, pneumonia, and chronic diarrhea were possibilities. These would require treatment by drugs.

The second type would be due to physical violence. One expects to suffer minor injuries such as cuts, abrasions, bruises, torn nails, and must be prepared to put up with them. One does not want a serious injury.

One could break a bone by falling or getting in the way of moving gear. One could have fingers or toes crushed by being trapped by moving ropes or pinched between moving parts of the boat. One could get severe rope burns or burns from cooking accidents. One could be concussed by being struck on the head by the boom.

I asked my brother-in-law, Geoff, for advice on a medical kit, and he provided me with a collection of drugs and instructions on their use. They were mainly antibiotics in various forms, and pain-killers, mild and strong. I also had some antisleep pills for those occasions when it would be necessary to stay awake. I had a first-aid kit packed in a shoe box. This contained bandages, burn dressings, plaster bandages for setting fractures, local anesthetic ampoules and syringes, and needles and thread for stitching wounds. I also had a roll of gauze from my grandfather's surgery. He stopped practicing medicine well over fifty years ago, but the roll was still in its original wrapper. Along with my old sextant it was the oldest thing on the boat.

As well as those emergency supplies, I had some vitamin and trace-element pills, which I took intermittently. I didn't expect to show signs of vitamin deficiency even without them, since it takes about six weeks for the symptoms to show. My food supply contained a fair supply of everything, but I occasionally took pills just in case.

Several people asked me why I didn't have my appendix removed, and if I wasn't worried about getting appendicitis. I have never understood why this should be such a common fear. Why should my appendix start complaining now, after twenty-eight years without trouble? Surely the chance of dying of appendicitis on this trip was not materially greater than the chance of dying on the operating table having it out as a precautionary measure. If I did have trouble, I had sufficient antibiotics to control the inflammation until a ship responded to a distress signal.

The next morning, Day 6, I got up at 0700 hours because I had a backache from lying down for so long. It was a beautiful morning; sunny with a few clouds and a crawling silver sea with a long Atlantic swell. There was a perfect breeze from the southwest and *Aziz* kept up a comfortable five knots. The horizon was very clear, and I got a good sextant sight in the morning and another at night to fix my position. For the first time I was east of the desired track to the Azores. This was because I had been on the southern track most of the previous day.

The system used to find one's position from the sun is as follows. Using a sextant you measure the angle made by a line from the sun to you and from the horizon to you. This is known as the altitude of the sun. If you know the time precisely and your position roughly, it is a simple matter to work out from tables the position of an imaginary line, the position line, at right angles to the sun's bearing from you, on which you are placed somewhere. By taking sights at different times of the day, when the sun's bearings are different, you can get two position lines, and the point where they cross is your precise position. Of course you have to allow for the distance traveled between taking the two sights.

The way I tried to work my sights was to take one in the morning when the sun was due east, from which I would get a position line that was my longitude. At noon, when the sun is due south, I would take another sight that would give me my latitude. I would plot these lines on the chart and move the longitude forward the distance I reckoned I had traveled. This gave me my position at noon.

Sometimes, of course, the sun would not be visible at the appropriate time. Then I would take sights when I could and cross the position lines for a fix, and from that work back or forward to a noon position.

All this was fun, and I always looked forward to doing my daily navigation. Occasionally I would take sights of the moon or planets, not because it was necessary but because they were so beautiful that it seemed a shame not to use them.

I was not feeling as bad as the day before, but was still headachy. I did not have a proper meal but ate snacks all day and sorrowfully contemplated the bond locker with all the booze and cigarettes in it, regretting that so far I hadn't felt like any debauchery.

I spent most of the day reading *The Elizabethan Epic* by Lacey Baldwin Smith. It was interesting, but I found that it was not detailed enough. Maybe I was too ignorant of the period to appreciate the background.

The interior of the boat was still rather a shambles.

I hadn't yet been able to get into the heads, or toilet compartment, as the swing of the door was stopped by all the boxes on the cabin floor. It didn't worry me very much as I went over the side of the boat instead, sticking my bottom over the lifelines and hanging on with both hands, which is just as good and really less trouble—you don't have to pump water in and out of the bowl. Actually, I never used the heads for the proper purpose.

I noted that it was about time I got the floorboards up and pumped the bilge out. But this would have to wait until I had reorganized the chaos on top of the boards somewhat. I didn't feel up to doing that.

During the afternoon, I passed through a patch of fragmented foam. I don't know what it was, but I imagine that it was some sort of pollution from a ship. I'm afraid that my own contribution to ocean pollution was greater than it should have been. I tried to make sure that all cans and bottles sank immediately but was careless with plastic. Ideally I should have kept it all for destruction on land, but I just threw it all over. One is not encouraged to make a great effort to keep half a dozen containers when one knows that the ocean liners discharge all their waste into the sea.

I saw very little evidence of pollution. I had only two small lumps of oil come aboard, though the mess they made was disproportionate to their size. I saw one or two floating bottles and an occasional small piece of wood. On the return from the Azores last year we had seen a lot of light bulbs floating past, Lord knows why. This time I didn't see any.

## Snags

At some time during the day, I crossed the track we had made last year from the Azores to the Scilly Isles. We had had a most frustrating passage with long periods of calm. But in this area we had been overtaken by a Force 9 gale. The waves had been long and high with breaking crests. We were frequently washed by waves, and one broke into the heavily reefed mainsail, ripping it from side to side. The wind blew at gale force for over a day, and we drifted about 60 miles due east. We were lucky to have plenty of sea room, for many unfortunate craft in British and French coastal waters were damaged and some foundered, trying to keep off the shore.

That evening, before retiring with a couple of aspirin, I took off the genoa and put on the No. 1 jib, for the wind had strengthened a little. I put about onto the port tack, making a course due west.

My procedure for changing foresails was then as follows:

1. Dress up in oilskin jacket and trousers and safety harness.
2. Get new sail and old bag out of after locker (the large locker with a round hatch behind the cockpit).
3. On to foredeck to tie bags to pulpit.
4. Back to cockpit to slacken off sheet.
5. To mast to uncleat halyard.
6. To bows holding halyard to catch sail as it drops.
7. Unhank and bag old sail.
8. Unbag and hank on new sail.

9. Clip on sheets and halyard.
10. Hoist new sail and cleat halyard.
11. To cockpit to tighten sheet.
12. To mast with winch handle to winch halyard taut and stow halyard tail.
13. Fetch sail bags from foredeck and stow in after locker.
14. Adjust sheet as necessary.
15. Adjust self steering as necessary.

The great majority of these sail changes could be made without altering the setting of the self-steering gear. *Aziz* was sufficiently responsive and the self-steering sufficiently powerful for a course to be held even when the sails were grossly unbalanced. This was a great advantage, for I found that in heavy weather *Aziz* would sail most courses with only a jib or a main.

The procedure sounds complicated but was in fact fairly simple, unless I inadvertently left out a step, which was a terrible nuisance as I usually had to go back to an earlier stage. I suppose it took about 20 minutes to start with, but soon I could do it much faster if the conditions weren't too bad. Wearing a safety harness slowed me down as I had to unclip and reclip the harness line three times to get from the cockpit to the bows. Sometimes I would trip over the line or get it wound around something. But I had promised my mother that I would wear it, so I did. I never wore a life jacket because I was afraid that if I did fall in it would be a handicap in those few moments when I might be able to get back on board. If I didn't get back and was left floating in the ocean, I wanted to

68

drown quickly rather than slowly, for there would be no chance of surviving.

After changing the sail, I lit the Tilley lamp and stood it on the step over the engine so that I could read by its light. And the inevitable happened: I knocked it off. The glass globe shattered on the floor, the mantle broke, and a jet of hot kerosene sprayed all over the place. I grabbed the thing, turned off the kerosene, and burned myself on the vaporizer. I dropped it again and cursed heartily. After regaining my composure I found the rubber-covered flashlight, and by its light picked up the fragments of glass and threw them overboard. Then I wiped up the kerosene and wedged the lamp on the floor.

I had solved the problem of keeping the lamp showing outside all night. I couldn't—without the glass the lamp would burn only in still air. I would just have to keep my fingers crossed and hope that I wouldn't get run down. In a way it was a relief, for I would be able to sleep more peacefully, not having to get up and pump the lamp at intervals. Fortunately I was well clear of the shipping lanes according to my chart.

It was a beautiful night, and without the lamp I could really see the milky phosphorescence. If I put my head over the side and looked back along the wake, it seemed like a runway rushing away, while from standing height it looked like a comet trail. I love phosphorescence and could spend hours hypnotized by the little lights rushing by.

The following morning, Day 7, I felt very much better and hardly had a headache. I looked at my watch to see what time it was and found that it had stopped. The inside of the glass was misted over, so I suppose that water had seeped in. I was upset because it had been reliable and easy to read. I had bought it the previous year at Beirut Airport, and it had served me faithfully and waterproofly throughout the Azores trip. I didn't have another watch but had a traveling alarm clock, a tin alarm clock, and the navigation chronometer, so I was not worried about not knowing the time.

During the morning I rearranged the boxes on the floor and pumped the bilge. The bilge pump was fitted in a stupid place, inside the heads compartment. I had to lift the floor boards, open the exit cock of the toilet, and put the exit pipe from the pump into the toilet bowl. I then worked the pump, which transferred water from the bilge to the bowl, from which it is supposed to run into the sea by gravity. This is all right when the boat is on an even keel or heeling to starboard, but when she is heeling to port the water will not run out and one must pump out the toilet as well. Not quite the system for an emergency. I was, however, carrying a portable gusher pump, which I kept in the after locker.

This time I had no trouble and got rid of a lot of murky water. This was good as *Aziz* had bounced about in the night and the bilge water had made the bottoms of several boxes soggy.

I also rigged an aerial for the radio by taking a wire on to one of the bolts from the mast step through the deck. It was difficult to get a good contact as there wasn't enough of the bolt showing for me to wrap the wire round it. I could only stick it on with insulating tape. Nevertheless reception was vastly improved, so I assumed that the mast was acting as an aerial. I could pick up BBC Radio 2 again and get the shipping forecasts, which were useful for the general synopsis of weather although I was now out of the forecast areas.

The wind started to rise, and for the first time I hoisted my new No. 3 jib, the smallest sail apart from the storm jib. It was really a working jib for a Folkboat, a 25-foot yacht, and was not quite the right shape for the Pionier as it needed the sheet taking further forward than I could manage to get the pull in the right direction. The solution was to raise the whole sail further up the forestay by putting an eighteen-inch strap between the foot of the sail and the deck. I resolved to do this when I had time but left the sail as it was for the time being.

This new jib had a very nice shape and showed up the other sails, which were rather baggy from use. I think I should have bought more new sails as I am sure I would have made better speed with flatter sails. I shall know better next time.

Next time?

"Day 8. 0730 hours. Have just got up to put about on to the port tack for a change. Now everything will gradually slide to the other side of the boat. Slept well last night but had vivid dreams of going to a big dinner party at a Berni-ish place which I knew was in Bristol, and having huge pieces of red beef cut by a mountaineer. At the time I thought I had done a clever rematerializing act because I knew *Aziz* was out here on the ocean. A second dream was of arriving at a hotel from off the boat with my parents and being given some letters and a first-class meal, but the most impressive thing was that they had three toilets all in one huge bathroom! I'm aFreud I'm going potty after all!"

I had a lot of vivid dreams while on *Aziz* and can remember quite a number of them. I usually dream a lot and thoroughly enjoy myself. I wonder if this is a necessary quality for staying happy when alone, for one gets stimulation from these dreams which is a substitute for external stimulation.

Both sky and sea were a steely gray, and *Aziz* was going well with small sails. I heard on the radio that the Navy had had a sad day. A sailing race from Plymouth to Fowey had been hit by a sudden gale and the boats had been scattered. Two men died, and ten were in the hospital.

I got very worried about my navigation. I took three sights in the morning, and the answer they gave seemed a long way out. After checking my calculations and trying to work out what could be wrong, I concluded that the sextant must be giving erroneous readings. I started by checking the index error. This is the difference between the angle of the sun above the horizon as read off the sextant and the true angle. I checked it by looking at the horizon and lining up the reflected image with the real image. If there was no error the sextant should read

0°00′. It is usual to have an error of about 0°05′ due to the mirrors being slightly out of parallel. Mine had an error of 0°40′! And I had been assuming an error of 0°06′. One minute of arc equals one nautical mile, so my positions were about 35 miles out. No wonder they didn't match up very well.

I reset the sextant by adjusting the angle of the mirror. At noon I took sights with that sextant and with an old one I had. This attractive instrument, which had a brass scale inlaid with silver, and a vernier scale for fine measurement, gave a much better image of the sun but was extremely difficult to read. The two instruments agreed, and I breathed a sigh of relief. I was still averaging over a hundred miles a day on the log, which is about 4¼ knots, so I was quite satisfied with my progress. Nevertheless I was still depressed about the navigation because I wasn't sure the sextant was the only problem.

It lifted my spirits to see my first shearwater.

## SIX

# Sailing Through the Spout

ONE OF THE pleasures of ocean voyaging is the enjoyment of natural things, of the abundant life of the sea, from the smallest plankton, visible only when it lights up with fear, to the great whales, to the birds that live on the open ocean and rarely touch down on the land.

The most common birds in the mid-Atlantic are petrels and shearwaters. Petrels are delightful little birds, dark brown with a flash of white above the forked tail. They flit to and fro across the waves, continually changing direction, searching for specks of food on the surface. Their feet hang down, and the birds look as though they

74

are dancing on the water. This is why they are called petrels, for St. Peter walked on the sea. In a mirror calm you can sometimes see the ripples when they touch the surface. In a howling gale you still see them, flying a few inches above the water, dodging the seas with amazing skill, rising above the crests to flit again into the hollows. My spirits responded to their joyful dance.

The shearwater is a less delicate bird. Greenish brown on top with a white underside, he curves and swoops in graceful swings from wave to wave. Like a gull following a plow, he searches the turbulent wake for scraps of food.

I spent a lot of time watching these birds, and regretted that I hadn't a camera good enough to record their beauty.

Although I am less than a third of the way across, I pick up an American show on the shortwave radio. It is a sort of "In Town Tonight" for New York, in which visitors to the city are interviewed. It seems a world away from *Aziz*, but I am sorry when it is ended, to be followed by dull pop music.

I start to wonder if I am changed in any way by being alone for a week. I feel the same; no happier, no more frightened, no more lonely. I do want to talk to someone and tell what has happened in the time since I left Dale, but don't feel distress because I can't. The radio is a great help as it keeps me in touch with reality.

I listened mainly to talk programs. There was not much music broadcast on the shortwave bands, and when there was some, reception was not good enough to make it worth listening to. But I enjoyed current affairs programs, news, discussions, and plays, not to mention commentaries on cricket, rugby, and tennis matches.

It is encouraging to hear an American program. It makes me feel that I am going somewhere, not just sailing into the unknown. I imagine what the seamen on Columbus' ships must have felt. They must have been terrified as they kept sailing toward the rim of the world, wondering what happened when you reached it. Would you fall off into oblivion? I bet the lookouts were on the ball.

But suppose I never see a ship nor any sign of an outside world? Will I mind? Do I miss human company? I think of the periods in my life when I have been far lonelier than I am now. But then I was lonely among people, now I am alone by myself.

My first recollection of loneliness is of my years at boarding school, where I was sent when I was eleven. At first I was very happy, full of confidence, looking forward to a new experience. After two weeks I was put up a class into one where I was the youngest. Some of the older girls were very unkind to me. No doubt they resented this new girl who was brighter than them. I couldn't understand it. No one had ever treated me like this, and I was completely unequipped to deal with such a situation. So I withdrew into myself and became a very solitary person, grateful when I was included in a group but without the courage to make the first approach.

I gradually modified this attitude as I grew older, but it returned when I went to the university. The difference here was that I soon had a boyfriend and did not have to make my own friends, we did everything together. After a year my confidence grew, and I dared express opinions of my own. Eventually we parted, and I went through the worst period of loneliness I have ever experienced. I knew practically nobody apart from mutual friends, and with those people I did know I was too proud to admit my loneliness outright and ask for company. I was still frightened of being rebuffed.

Then it dawned on me that I had been too inward-looking and hadn't considered that other people might suffer from similar fears. I realized that if you are friendly to people they are likely to be friendly in return. But you can't expect them to make the first move, and you must respond clearly to any move that is made. It worked wonders. Since then I have had much less difficulty with personal relationships and have had no long bouts of loneliness and despair.

Even so I had acquired the habit of solitude and cannot do without it. I get very wrought up if I cannot have time alone. So I was not appalled by the thought of being alone.

I thought of the future.

"It is a funny thing to think of a future which may not exist and, if it does, is ill defined. For example, I don't know what tomorrow will hold for me—will it be another gray day with no sun and no excitement, or will it be a heavenly day or will it be a fearful day? And if fearful, man-made or nature-made fears?"

It was a curious feeling. This was the first time I had recognized the nonexistence of the future. Until something happens it does not exist. We can imagine that it exists in the future, but this is a mere technique of thinking, reflected in our language, just as imaginary numbers are only a technique of calculation. It is, of course, possible to construct an image of tomorrow, store it in the mind, and compare it with reality when tomorrow is now. Most people have sufficiently well-ordered lives to obtain a good match. But isn't it fun when something unforeseeable occurs? Isn't this the real pleasure of living? If it were not so, we could exist entirely in our minds, never looking out at the world and never taking new ideas from other minds. Perhaps some people can do this. I can't. I need stimulation from other people.

So we come back to loneliness. Why did I think that I could face six weeks without interaction with the world of people? Because I planned it, I expected it, and I expected it to end. I would not be lonely, for that is a state in which you wish for a relationship with some person. I had relationships which I knew were continuing. I was thinking of my friends, and I knew they were thinking of me. But if I were flung into isolation without preparation and without hope, I would be lonely, and might despair. To be taken from life and thrown into prison without hope of release would be appalling. But to be in mid-Atlantic in my own boat with books, radio, food, and drink, through my own choice, is rather enjoyable. So long as nothing goes wrong.

I had now settled to a pattern of eating which rather amused me. I had always maintained that the human body is badly designed with regard to fuel requirements. It would be much better to eat only once every two days, and then do it really well so as to satisfy the esthetic side without being surfeited. Surely this is preferable to eating ordinary food every few hours just to satisfy one's energy requirements. The odd thing was that now that I had complete freedom to eat as I wished, I spent much of the day nibbling away at little bits of this and that. I think this must be because I had so little to occupy myself that food became a major source of experience.

In the morning I would have a bowl of muesli, a mixture of oatmeal, cereal, nuts, raisins and apple flakes. Add milk, and the mixture swells to make a nourishing and filling meal. I was using Ever Ready milk, which is heat-treated so that it will last unopened for months. My cartons were dated for use by November 11, 1971, so I didn't expect to have trouble with its going sour. It tastes foul in tea, but otherwise it's all right.

During the morning I would probably eat some fruit, an apple while they lasted, or a carrot or an orange. I might well have some cheese or some of my mother's homemade cookies. Around noon I would have a can of shrimp, sardines, or Spam, or perhaps an egg with mayonnaise, followed by cheese or fruit and a can of beer. At teatime, I would have a mug of China tea with a slice of lemon accompanied by a considerable number of cookies or a few slices of cake.

In the evening I had a hot meal of some sort. Macaroni Bolognese *à la Aziz* was a favorite. I made this by slicing and frying an onion, adding a can of ground meat

79

and stirring it around for a minute or two, then adding a little water, a fair bit of tomato paste, a bay leaf, salt and pepper and a handful of quick macaroni. Simmer for 20 minutes and you have a tasty dish. Because my onions were large and my cans of ground meat full size I always ended up with vast quantities. I usually had to give some to the fish, but sometimes I would wade through the lot and then fall back in a stupor. I never got bored with food, for I had a good variety on board. I had such vast quantities that I ate only the things I really liked and didn't have to face the unappetizing things like stewed steak.

Cooking was usually quite easy, even when the weather was rough, because the gas burner was pivoted so that it would remain horizontal as the boat rolled. Next to the burner was a sink which I used as temporary storage for implements which were not in immediate use. I did not use it for washing as it was easier to use a bucket in the cockpit. All dirty dishes and cutlery were put in the bucket, and when I felt inclined I washed them with sea water and liquid detergent. I washed myself in the same way, in sea water. I did not want to waste any of my 40 gallons of fresh water, and once you start washing in it the precious fluid soon vanishes.

All the food was stowed in the forward cabin, except for immediate use supplies which were behind the galley. On the evening of the ninth day, I was getting a can from the collection in the central well when I noticed that there was a pool of blue liquid in each of the side wells. I smelled it and discovered that it was kerosene, which must have leaked from the yellow cans. Nothing seemed to be damaged except two books that had somehow got mixed in with the stores, so I fished out the kerosene cans and put them in the cockpit before mopping up the mess with a sponge and bucket.

When I examined the cans, I found that they were not holed but that the leak was from the caps. The rubber washers had swollen and were rumpled up inside the cap. I decided to cut them to size and had just got out the scissors when I was surprised by a noise.

"Hshwhewou!" Like an engine letting off steam.

"What the devil's that?" I thought. It was like the sound of dolphin's breathing vastly magnified. It must be a whale.

I leaped up quickly and looked about. Despite the settling dusk I could see a smooth patch of sea gently seething 100 yards away from the port bow. Then came another "Hshwhewou" from the other side. I jerked my head round and saw a spout of mist hanging above a shiny dark back that sank slowly beneath the water. Then I heard an even louder blow, and the first whale rolled out of the sea a mere 50 feet from *Aziz*. My heart thumped, for this was just too close. "Mind my boat." I imagined the thump, the dreadful lurching, the snapping of the rigging, the gushing of the water over me as one of these huge beasts surfaced under me. "For Christ's sake, mind me."

The second whale surfaced and blew a little further away, followed by the first a few hundred yards to my left. And again, to right and left of me, then in front, like great dolphins. "Thank heavens, they do know I'm here!" My agitation subsided, and I settled down to watch the show. First I would hear the blow and, looking around, see the spout rising 15 feet or more into the air and gradually dispersing down wind. A long, long, muddy brown back would roll under the spout, and eventually a fin would break the surface. Then the creature would gently sink away, leaving a smooth, eddying patch of water to mark its excursion. I never saw head nor tail, but since the visible part must have been over 30 feet long, I guessed that the total would be over 50 feet. The weight would therefore be between 50 and 75 tons, compared with *Aziz*'s 3½ tons.

I sailed through the spout of one. This is the exhaled breath, and I had read that it smells particularly fetid. This hardly smelled at all, just a warm moist air. I noticed bits of red-orange stuff floating in the blow patch but could not imagine what this could be.

I think these must have been sperm whales. That is the type they catch in the Azores, harpooning them by hand from open boats, a heroic but bloody business.

After the pleasure my whales had given me, I didn't want them to end up that way.

# SEVEN

# A Thousand Miles Away

THE NEXT morning, Day 10, I was worried again about my navigation. I took a number of sights that did not agree very well. The general opinion was that I was east of my last position, which was a very odd result since I had been making a course well to the west of south and the current was not supposed to be at all strong. I should have worked out a dead reckoning position but stupidly didn't, mainly because I had left behind the graph paper on which to draw the distance since the previous fix. Even so, I could recognize a stupid answer when I got one.

I sat down in a huff and started to read one of my navigation books to see if I could get an idea of what had gone wrong. Suddenly it dawned on me that it is possible to use the Consol position fixing system without having the special Consol charts, if you have the appropriate *Admiralty List of Radio Signals*, which is Volume 5.

Consol is a system designed for aircraft navigation and is not very accurate, but one would expect to be within 20 miles which was good enough for me. It works like this: each Consol transmitting station—there are five in Europe—sends out a radio signal which consists of a number of dots followed by a number of dashes, or vice versa. The number of dots and dashes—the total is always 60—depends on the observer's bearing from the transmitter. All you have to do is count the dots and dashes and look up the tables which give number of dots or dashes against bearing. If you use two or three stations you get bearings that you can cross for a position.

I got the radio tuned in quickly and picked up Ploneis, which is in Brittany, and Lugo, which is in northern Spain. The signals were faint as I was at extreme range, and I had difficulty counting the dots. However, I managed to reach the same figure on several counts, and duly worked out a position. This turned out to be farther north than I thought I was.

At noon I got a meridian altitude, which gave me a position about a hundred miles south of the Consol fix. This seemed more likely, and in the afternoon I got another sight which, when crossed with the noon sight and suitably adjusted for course and distance run since noon, gave a position that I was happy to believe, though I wasn't a hundred percent convinced.

I did quite a bit of writing in my diary. "1315. I am sitting here smoking and drinking brandy and smelling gorgeous, as I have just daubed myself with scent to cheer myself up. I think that living on this boat is like moving into a new flat. For the first week or so one hasn't enough to do apart from look after the place, but after a while one settles down and is able to while away the hours doing very little. *Aziz* is doing well, and I am a bit ashamed of the chaos inside, but by now it is a more organized chaos and I know where to find everything (I think)."

You will have gathered that I am not an obsessively tidy person but am happy if my chaos is organized and I know where everything is. The cabin would have offended many sailors because it was apparently a shambles. In fact, it was logically stowed for one person. There were boxes on the floor containing carbonated drink, fruit, chandlery, and cordage, there was a large tin containing homemade cake, and there was the spare battery which made a useful coffee table. Also on the floor were the permanently damp things, safety harness and oilskin jacket and trousers.

Under the table which bridges the settee was the equipment that was in frequent use or might be needed quickly: the signal lamp, the distress radio, the loud-hailer, the cameras, and my spectacles, all jammed tight with books and my handbag. Jeans and towels hung over the heads door, and a sweater huddled in the corner of the settee. I can see the expression on the face of many a proud boat owner.

The area behind the gas ring and sink was choc-a-bloc with packets and bottles of pickles, herbs, spices, curry powder, instant coffee, tea, mayonnaise, cooking oil, vinegar, salt, pepper, mustard, vitamin pills, lemon juice, sugar, rice, oatmeal, muesli, orange squash, whisky, and brandy. And other things. All was packed solid so that it would not rattle about. On a shelf above were mugs, bowls, and more food containers. In the locker beneath were pans, bottles of spirits, cigarettes, and bottles of methyl alcohol for starting the Tilley lamp.

It would have been impossible for a stranger, but this chaos was my chaos, created with my own hands, and I liked it.

I did not have the luxury of a chart table and did all my plotting with the chart on the windward settee, kneeling on the floor or sitting on the cake tin. It was difficult at times to keep my balance when *Aziz* was pounding to windward, and so the accuracy of my plotting was not up to ocean racing standards.

"I feel that I should be developing some grand philosophy of life, being all alone with plenty of time to think. But I don't feel any different, or more inclined to soul searching, than usual. Of course, with a basically humanistic, hedonistic philosophy like mine, I don't feel any real guilt and therefore no necessity for justification. In spite of being alone with the natural elements, I do not feel closer to a personal god. Rather I feel that I am another piece of flotsam (or jetsam) subject to natural forces. Only when I am frightened do I think of a personal deity, and that is (*a*) human and (*b*) cheating. One must live by one's beliefs and involve God equally when happy and when frightened. I must say that natural beauty gives me a sense of gratitude to the Creator—whom I do believe in."

This is a fair statement of my beliefs. When I was in my late teens and early twenties I counted myself a Christian, read books about Christianity, went to church, gave my tithe to the collection, and tried to behave as a Christian ought. It made me feel rather miserable because much of the time I could not honestly feel that I needed forgiveness: even when I had done something that I knew was wrong I could not truly ask to be forgiven. I knew that if the same circumstances arose again I would behave in a similar manner. In other words I suffered from guilt. It was not the guilt of having done wrong but the guilt of knowing I must be doing wrong—no man is perfect—but not believing it.

I eventually gave up trying to be a Christian because I knew that my behavior would not change and that I would be happier without this guilt about not feeling guilty.

So why is it that when danger threatened I called on God for help, a god whom I do not believe in, for my god is an observer of people, not a participant in human affairs. The call is forced out in desperation, to relieve the mind of the strain of keeping the whole person in balance. It is not made in a religious spirit, with faith that it might be effective. So when I say I prayed, I am misleading you. I know what prayer should be, and my cries did not resemble prayer in any meaningful way.

Since ceasing to call myself a Christian, I have had much more peace of mind. I have worked out a system of living which involves doing exactly what I want to do. This is actually quite difficult, for I have to decide what I really want to do deep down and the consequences of such an action, the possible hurt to other people and therefore to me. To make a decision on this basis requires considerable analysis of these consequences and is excellent exercise for the mind. But when I can reach no clear resolution of a conflict I make a decision on an emotional basis. The most foolproof method I have discovered for doing this is to toss a coin, but instead of abiding by the fall of the coin I note my reaction to the choice it has made and can thus determine which alternative I really want to follow.

It is in working out the consequences of an action that conscience comes in. It is conscience that stops us all from being selfish, grabbing, inconsiderate barbarians. Conscience is the learned set of values of a culture that enables people to live together in reasonable harmony. It is the civilizing factor. And, man being what he is, there is not only absence of guilt but also positive pleasure in obeying the strictures of conscience since mental tension is reduced.

It is therefore essential that children be taught the values of the society into which they are born so that when they become pleasure-seeking adults instead of pain-avoiding children they will still be able to maintain naturally an overtly unselfish mode of behavior. Indeed some of their pleasure will be derived from this sociable pattern of behaving. But unless they know the values of society, how can they question them constructively?

I had fun filling the compass that afternoon. When I dropped the boltcroppers on the glass, I had sealed the crack with flexible sealer. Somehow I had rubbed some of it off and a small leak must have developed for the bubble in the glass had become very large. The liquid is present in the compass bowl to slow down the oscillations of the needle due to the boat's motion. An undamped needle would be useless on a boat as it would spin around like a mad thing, never settling long enough for one to find out where it is pointing. I don't know how the early mariners managed with their pieces of lodestone on a string.

The liquid remaining in my compass was still covering the needle-mounted card to serve its damping function, but the bubble was so large that because of peculiar refraction through the three media of liquid, air, and glass, it was difficult to read the numbers on the card.

I took the compass off its bracket and looked for the filling hole. This was stopped up with a large screw under which were written the words FILL ONLY WITH ALCOHOL. Now that presented a problem for I hadn't brought any clear alcohol along, not even a bottle of gin. I did have whisky and brandy. I just hoped that one of these, diluted by the liquid still in the compass, would be transparent enough to let me read the card. I decided to try. If it did not work, I still had the telltale compass which I could mount in the cockpit.

I got out the brandy bottle, gripped the compass between my knees, unscrewed the filler screw and poured. An airlock promptly formed, and brandy streamed all over my trousers. I tried again more gently and managed to fill it up, though more brandy went over my trousers than in the compass. Still, I had another five bottles of the stuff. I finished by injecting the last few drops with a hypodermic syringe, and when I righted the compass I found that the bubble was tiny, a mere shadow of its former self. The card was now legible through the peat-colored liquid. I fixed the compass back in its bracket and decided to use the remainder of the brandy for its proper purpose.

As I sat there drinking my brandy and lemonade cocktail I started thinking about Donald Crowhurst again. He died at sea, having pretended that he was sailing round the world when he really hadn't left the Atlantic. I hadn't read the book about him; the more people said to me, "You must read about Donald Crowhurst," the less I wanted to read it, feeling that it might be bad luck. All I knew was that he had left Teignmouth, on the south coast of England, in a trimaran to compete in the Round the World solo race. He had quickly discovered that some essential equipment had been left behind and that his boat was not sufficiently seaworthy to face the Roaring Forties, but instead of turning back he had carried on, sending out misleading messages which implied that he was doing well in the race, when he never actually left the Atlantic. His trimaran was eventually found abandoned, and it was assumed that he had committed suicide.

The story disturbed me, as it was clear evidence of the mental stress of single-handed sailing.

"He must have been very upset before he left, since being alone tends to emphasize emotions already felt. I can understand the tendency to want to cheat—I feel it myself—but think he must have had terrific financial and emotional liabilities to be overcome by the temptation. If I had been he, I would hope to have kept my nerve and staged a dramatic shipwreck, so as to keep the goodies, the glory, and my life. Or would I? Perhaps I too would do the decent thing and say goodby to life honorably. But I think I am enough of a realist and a sufficiently good self-deceiver to get away with cheating."

I have now read the book about the voyage. They say he went mad, but by whose definition? Surely madness can only be defined as an inability to deal with one's surroundings, and Crowhurst was clearly capable of doing that. Certainly he was not "normal"; his attitude to life changed drastically, and it is probable that he did commit suicide. But one could argue that this is evidence of sanity, of an awareness that this was the best solution to his problems, in the long run. It is not long since suicide was expected of a man who had got into personal or financial difficulties, and I think that Donald Crowhurst was brave enough to do it.

But if he intended to live he should never have ventured on this voyage without more time to get ready. His boat was ill prepared and his reasons for going were wrong. He showed that he was not able to plan and organize effectively, and planning and organization are the basis of success in anything.

They said that I should not have gone. If I drowned they would have said I was foolhardy; if Crowhurst had succeeded they would have said he was a hero. Nothing succeeds like success: nothing fails like failure.

With such dismal thoughts I went to bed. At 0430 hours I passed the 1,000-mile mark on the log. By the following morning I could steer the course I wanted to take me between Terceira and São Miguel as the wind had veered during the night. By noon it was near enough a calm, and I decided to go up the mast to get the radar reflector down so that I could do something about its sharp edges. I rigged the bosun's chair and was just hauling myself up when along came a breeze and off we went. Without taking the mainsail down I could not get a grip on the mast with my knees and so was banged around. So down I came, without the reflector. "I have just discovered how to end a calm. Climb the mast."

I noticed that my good alarm clock had stopped. I opened it up to have a look inside. (I can't resist opening things to see how they work.) Alas! In reassembling it I made an error and ensured that if it hadn't been irrevocably broken before, it was now. Still, the cheap alarm, and the chronometer were working—two down and two to go!

Becalmed again during the afternoon, I pottered around the deck with nothing on, soaking up the first bit of sunshine for days. I did a bit of washing and hung the clothes on one of the lifelines where it looked very gay. Then I relaxed over tea with bread and honey, followed by some of my mother's parkin. Later on, I ate a whole packet of cheese-spread triangles and a couple of tomatoes, and only after finishing did I remember that I was supposed to be having a celebration dinner that night to mark the thousand miles from home.

I remembered our celebration last year for 1,000 miles out from the Azores. We had curried steak and rice, accompanied by Portuguese champagne. That was the last good meal we had as by then we were on strict rations. It was the last meat that Peter and I had, for the third member of the crew, Mike Robertson, is allergic to fish and eggs, so he got all the steak and Spam while we had the eggs—very dubious—and canned tuna fish. This time I had planned the meal before I left. I was to have shrimp cocktail, asparagus, ham, new potatoes, and lichis.

After all my nibbling, I couldn't face the thought of a big meal so I postponed it to the next evening.

When I woke the following morning and looked out of the cabin, I could see a line of black clouds approaching. I decided that it might be a good idea to replace the genoa with the next size down, the No. 1 jib. Thank goodness I did, for 20 minutes later we were hit by the most impressive squall I had ever experienced. The rain came down solidly, flattening the sea and soaking my trousers in a split second. I had to leap to the helm, for *Aziz* was pressed over. I bore away from the wind and ended up sailing northeast at a great rate—in the direction of Britain. I gybed round and shot off south by east instead, the sky full of rain and the sea whipped up into little white horses.

As I sat there heaving on the tiller, for the sails were not trimmed properly, I felt the strain die away. The air became air again, light penetrated the sky, and the white horses lay down. Soon all was peaceful; I brought *Aziz* back on to the wind, and we sailed on toward the Azores.

By late afternoon it was very calm, and I motored for an hour to loosen up the engine and charge the battery. I dislike motoring intensely; the noise shatters the peace of a calm sea, the boat vibrates, and I have to concentrate very hard on the steering compass. A moment's inattention is enough to allow *Aziz* to whip round in a semicircle. She has practically no directional stability because she has a short keel and a separate rudder. This means that she is maneuverable and easily handled by the self-steering gear and by me. But it also means that she is a pig under power, and God help me if the self-steering breaks. I would have a job rigging a makeshift system and would probably end up steering eighteen hours a day—a nasty thought.

Trying to get a cigarette and matches out of the cabin is quite a laugh. I center the tiller so she is steering straight, climb into the cabin, stretch out to straighten her up again, duck down to open the match locker, stretch out again to straighten her, grab the fags, and leap back into the cockpit. Why didn't I throttle back so that *Aziz* was almost still? Because I was enjoying myself—a sort of "beat the machine" game.

A nice breeze picked up early in the night, and we went belting along slightly off the wind with the genoa doing a grand job. The breeze dropped a little in the morning, but we still moved along fairly well under a gray, overcast sky.

At noon I took a sight. "I can't believe it. My noon sight—taken with both sextants—puts me at 40°46′N, which is well north of what I thought. I fear my navigation may be completely adrift—I can't pick up the Azores beacons. I might be anywhere. It is most worrying. I keep taking sights but no longer believe them. Oh, woe! I just can't be up there."

At 1500 hours I happened to look out of the cabin, and what did I see?

A ship—a ship at last. Thank goodness—I had begun to doubt that they existed. This one is about two miles away, already abeam, a gray silhouette moving steadily east against a gray haze. Quick as a flash I get out the signal lamp and gaily send off AA AA AA—the call-up signal. No reply. He *must* see me. I flash again K K K—"I wish to communicate with you." Still no reply, and now he is going away from me. Again I try, but it is no good. My heart sinks, and a tear of frustration and despair comes into my eyes. "It's not fair. Why isn't he looking?" But of course it is fair: I had spotted him too late.

Will it be another thirteen days before I see the next ship? I hope not. I do want to get a message back to my parents so that they will know I am still alive. I expect they are pretty worried at not having heard anything, particularly because I told them that I expected to talk with a ship at least once a week. Let's hope I can get a message through when I get to the Azores.

# EIGHT

# Temptation One

I WAS NOW getting close to the Azores, I thought, and at last I managed to get radio Direction Finding bearings on the beacons on São Miguel and Santa Maria.

The Azores are a group of nine volcanic islands rising steeply from the sea. There are three groups. The southern pair of Santa Maria and São Miguel are the most important from an international point of view, for Santa Maria has the international airport and São Miguel has the capital city, Ponta Delgada. About 100 miles west northwest of São Miguel is the middle group, consisting of Terceira, Graciosa, Pico, São Jorge, and Fayal, and about 100 miles northwest of these are the northern pair, Florez and Corvo.

The islands were uninhabited until the Portuguese colonized them in the fifteenth century. Then they became a rendezvous for the Spanish and Portuguese fleets on their way back from the New World. Consequently they were the scene of a number of battles between the English, greedy for plunder, and the Peninsular powers.

It was off Florez that the famous battle between Sir Richard Grenville in the little *Revenge* and 53 Spanish ships of war took place. The *Revenge* fought bravely, becalmed in the lee of a great galleon, but surrendered after fighting for 15 hours. The English considered it a great battle and a moral victory. English children are still taught about it in school.

The islands are now friendly to the British, and we had a great welcome when we visited them last year. We arrived in Ponta Delgada ten days out from Spain and spent a week there, the crew sightseeing and the captain selling seed potatoes. São Miguel is the largest of the islands and, like the others, is covered with little green and yellow walled fields climbing the sides of volcanic hills. The roads are lined with blue hydrangeas and are traveled by as many horses and mules as cars.

After a week we sailed to Fayal, the most perfect sail I ever had. The sky was blue, the sea was sapphire, the wind was just right. We sunbathed all day and lazily watched the seas go past. Navigation was easy, for the positions of the islands were clearly marked by the cap of cloud over each. Nevertheless I was relieved when Pico and São Jorge duly appeared from under their bonnets, for this was the first time I had been in charge of navigation.

During the night we sailed between these two islands, craning our necks to peer at the top of Pico, a perfect volcanic cone reaching 7,600 feet. We arrived at Horta, the port of Fayal, the following morning. There were several yachts tied up there, most of them en route to Europe from the West Indies but some having come the same way as us. In our ten days there we swam, saw the sights, drank in the Café Sport, and visited São Jorge. We had a terrific welcome there; it seemed as if the whole town was on the quayside. Every move we made was commented on, and despite the language problem we were shown over the island.

We then went to Santa Cruz on Florez. This had the most terrifying harbor it has been my misfortune to spend a night in. To enter the harbor you head for a narrow gap in the volcanic reef and, as soon as you are through, turn sharply to starboard. If you don't make this turn, you end up on the cliffs, as did one British yacht whose bones are still visible. The harbor is tiny and a big swell comes in. We were moored with two lines to buoys and two lines around pinnacles of rock. *Pinta* would surge toward the rocks. Our hearts would stop. Then she would surge back toward the center of the harbor. We stayed for one sweaty night. In the morning we took in the lines from the rocks, cut the lines to the buoys and motored out to head for home. Was I glad to leave!

This time I was going to keep clear of land but wanted to sight one of the islands to check my position. I could not decide whether to pass between the middle and southern groups or whether to go south of the lot. If you study the winds and currents, the situation looks slightly more favorable if one goes south. But it is farther, and on balance I thought it would be better to pass between. However, the wind was southwesterly, and unless it changed I would have to tack to get north of São Miguel, which would hardly be worthwhile. I decided to keep as far west as possible and see how it panned out.

As usual, I spent the day nibbling and listening to the radio. The news was full of the Common Market negotiations, with a statement to be made in the House of Commons about them. I became terribly well informed about such issues as I was picking up programs from all over the world—Britain, America, Canada, South Africa, Australia, and Russia. There was also a splendid religious station broadcasting from, I think, Ecuador, which did fascinating interpretations of the Scriptures.

From my position well away from it all, I felt more objective about world events. I eventually decided that it would probably be a good thing if Britain joined the Common Market so that she would have a say in political and economic decisions which will affect her anyway. I also wished that they would think of another topic for discussion.

The following morning, Day 14, a radio DF fix put me about 100 miles from São Miguel. I needed to steer a course of 252° True to pass north of the island, but unfortunately the best I could make was 230° True, which was a nuisance. I decided to carry on and if necessary pass south of the island rather than put in a tack to the northwest. During the day the wind piped up a fraction, and I was making good speed with the No. 1 jib and a single reef in the main. We were pounding as the bows dropped off the tops of waves. Twice I got dressed and went out to change to a smaller jib, but each time I decided that the pounding was unavoidable because there was a little short sea.

By 1700 hours we were 40 miles from São Miguel, and the wind had backed 10° or so, which meant I would certainly have to go south of the island. I slept for a couple of hours in the afternoon in preparation for a night of watching for a light on the land. At dusk I took an antisleep pill, lit the Tilley lamp, and settled down to read *Lord of the Rings*. The sunset was splendid, with orange and russet overhanging the horizon and a pencil-thin silver crescent drawn on a deep blue sky.

At 0145 hours I sighted a light, bearing 241° True. This was the right bearing for the light on the northeast corner of São Miguel. I had made a correct landfall. The date was June 26, and I had been at sea for 13½ days, so I had made quite a reasonable passage.

The night was pitch black, the sky studded with brilliants. A perfect night for picking up lights. I saw the lights of a ship going east and wondered where he was going. I sailed steadily on and passed about 10 miles from the light, close enough to see the lines of street lamps in the town below the light and to watch a car's lights climb up and away.

At dawn we were still close, but cloud had formed, and instead of a yellow and green jewel rising from the sea there was a blue-gray shadow squatting under a gray cloud. Nevertheless out came the camera to record the scene and prove that I really had been there. I was delighted to have made a landfall and gained conclusive evidence that I was going somewhere, and the right somewhere at that.

Once clear of the land I wanted to head west for America. I couldn't because the wind was coming from the west, so I continued on the same course, down toward Santa Maria. This soon appeared as another gray shadow. I was pleased to have sighted Santa Maria, for now I had seen all the islands in the Archipelago Dos Açores.

"I am surprised how little tempted I am to close land and have a look at it. I would have liked to see the green and yellow strip fields and the little volcanic peaks, but all I can see is a blue-gray outline of both islands. . . . This is the end of Stage 1 and the beginning of Stage 2, which involves going due west for about 40° of longitude. . . . I wish I had been able to pass a message as I'm afraid my parents will be worrying."

I had actually gone to the length of writing a message addressed to the harbor master and putting it in a Tupperware box with a couple of packets of cigarettes. I hoped that I would be able to give it to a passing fishing boat, so naturally I didn't see any sort of vessel at all. I was regularly flown over by the ferry plane from Santa Maria to São Miguel and each time waved furiously. I imagined the passengers seeing my little boat beneath them and wondering where I was going. They wouldn't guess that I was heading for America.

I tacked between the islands and headed back toward São Miguel. The wind was very light by now, so I lowered the mainsail to do a few repairs. The second batten pocket had worn through at the inner end. I mended it by putting a layer of adhesive sail tape over it, then stitching a square of terylene cloth over that and finally putting another layer of tape round the edges of the patch. This took quite a long time as the cloth was stiff and I was in an awkward position on the cabin roof.

All the battens were broken except the first, and I replaced them. I had to cut a new second batten from a length of Tufnol-type strip. From being stowed bent in the forward cabin this had a bend in it, which gave the sail an odd shape. I hoped it would straighten out, and within a few hours it did.

At 1830 hours I was close again to São Miguel and through the binoculars I could clearly see Ponta Delgada. I thought of the good times we had had there last year, of the hospitable pilots, the good food, the lazy days. I was tempted to go close to see if I could pass a message, but did not dare. I could just imagine what might happen. "I'll just go a little closer to have a look," and then "I'll just sail around the harbor," and then, before I knew what had happened, I would be sitting in a café drinking a glass of wine. No! I resolutely put *Aziz* on to the other tack and headed away from land.

I slept like a log that night and woke at 0600 hours feeling very well. It was a sparkling day with a milky blue sea and a few clouds over where the islands must be. The wind had veered, and I was actually able to sail due west, which made me very happy.

In the morning I washed my hair, taking a couple of photographs of the process. I filled the bucket with sea water, put it on the cockpit floor, and stood in the cabin leaning out into the cockpit. When I had finished I rinsed about a pint of fresh water through my hair to get rid of the salt. The result was marvelous. I felt like a new woman. I then did some sunbathing, trying to get an all-over tan: it is cooler and more comfortable sunbathing naked, but I soon got a bit burned, so I gave up the life of the idle rich and went back to work.

I hauled myself up the mast to get the radar reflector down so that I could give it an antichafe treatment. It was rather nice up there, and I got a new view of *Aziz*. I could see her below me idly nosing through the wavelets. She looked like a broad white dart moving graciously beneath my feet, quite at ease with her world.

I took the radar reflector into the cabin where I bound the edges with two layers of insulating tape, topped with a layer of thin green plastic tape to stop the black stickiness of the insulating tape from dirtying the sails. I put extra layers over the corners and was quite pleased with the result. It used a lot of tape but was worth it if it stayed on. I had a hell of a struggle getting the thing reattached to the shrouds. I needed three hands for getting the last shackle pin in; one to hold the reflector, one to hold the shroud, and the third to hold the pin. Once I dropped the pin to the deck and had to go down to pick it up. I found I was getting quite tired when I hauled myself up again. Damn thing! I couldn't get it in; my arms were aching and my fingers were thumbs. I was just about to give up and fetch some wire to use instead when—presto!—there it was, all together and shipshape. I lowered myself to the deck, feeling virtuous, for the radar reflector had been on my conscience for a long time.

I saw some dolphins in the distance leaping above the horizon and splashing down in a fountain of white spray. I whistled to them to come closer, but they had business elsewhere. I love dolphins because they are so joyful, leaping about with such abandon.

I still had caught no fish despite trailing a line most of the time. I had lost several lures—a spinner, a spoon, and a plastic worm—so I knew that there were big fish about. Still, what would I do with a 200-pound tuna?

The next morning I found myself absolutely stationary under a brilliant sky. I soon discovered that I had company, a large school of little fish which gathered round the boat. The sea was clear and I could see, suspended beneath me, small organisms and jelly fish. The log line hung like a plumb line into the deeps.

The sun was very hot, and I stripped off to potter about the deck, photographing the fish and trying to catch one. They were very inquisitive and would rush up to inspect every tidbit I offered them. Clearly they were fish of discrimination, for everything I offered was turned down: cheese, rice, tomato, steak, and cookies. The school grew and grew in size until I felt as though I were sailing in a hatchery. Most of the fish flicked lazily to and fro, but one appeared to have something wrong, for it swam furiously on the surface leaving a trail of ripples. I wondered at first if it was some sort of courtship dance, but eventually concluded that it had sunstroke.

I enjoyed that day of idling around. I didn't mind being becalmed. I had expected it, and had had plenty of experience of drifting around with no power. On the return trip from the Azores, we recorded only one-fifth of a mile on the log one day. Coming back from Ireland two weeks before leaving on this trip, I had been becalmed and spent a night and a day drifting round the islands off the Pembrokeshire coast. That had been nerve-racking for the tides run strongly there, and at one time I thought I was going to end up on the rocks.

The next day, which was pretty calm, I spent painting the iron bracket supporting the self-steering vane. I had put several coats of metallic primer on at Dale but had not had time for a top coat. Now I painted it white, which smartened up the ugly structure some. It was quite a job, for I had to contort myself to reach all the parts without falling over. I succeeded in getting white streaks in my hair but managed to avoid spilling the paint over the deck.

There was a light following wind, so I raised twin foresails and dropped the main. The foresails, held outstretched by poles, seemed to be effective. *Aziz* was yawing about a lot because the wind was too light to swing the self-steering vane until we were a long way off course. One really wants to increase the vane area in these conditions, and I think an extension would be worthwhile if one expected a lot of downwind sailing. It would not be difficult to fix up. Then, why didn't I do it? My brain must have been addled by the sun.

I heard on the radio that day that Chay Blyth had completed his technical circumnavigation, crossing his outward track somewhere southwest of the Cape Verde Islands. He had sailed the "wrong" way around against the Roaring Forties. That must have been quite a trip.

The following morning there was sadder news: The three Russian cosmonauts who had been longer in space than any others had died during re-entry. What a tragedy. Just think of doing all that and never being able to tell what it was like.

I counted my unread books and found that I still had over a dozen left. I seemed to be getting through about one a day as there was a lot of time to fill in, a problem I had not anticipated. "In fact, although I am not lonely, I do get rather bored and could do with someone to talk to. Thank goodness for the radio. I think I would go potty without it, but think I am quite sane now, though becoming more impulsive over little things than before while more thoughtful about bigger things. Perhaps I am just getting a better sense of proportion."

During the night the wind rose to a sturdy Force 4–5 from the southwest, and a large swell appeared. By noon the next day I was down to the No. 2 jib and three reefs in the main. It was a most frustrating day: I couldn't sail close to the wind without great hammerings and slammings, and so I spent the day going north and south and not getting very far west. I made a tactical error here: I should have stuck to the southern tack and made some southing instead of trying to stay in the same latitude. I was a little too far north, too near the main flow of the Gulf Stream; I would have done better to keep away from it.

The bows were dipping under the water at times, water flooded over the foredeck up the cabin roof, and quite large lumps ended up in the cabin. The forehatch was leaking, and I could see dollops of water spurting through on to the stores. I made a mental note to put some sealer around the edges of the hatch when the foredeck was dry.

During the night I had a vivid dream about going ashore on Florez to send a message home. It did not look like Florez but was more like one of the Shetland

Isles, with great cliffs rising out of a ruff of spray. I went into the Post Office, but they wouldn't accept my English money. Then I found myself in a tiny shop trying to buy a packet of Gaulois cigarettes. They had shelves and shelves of them in various colored packets, but none in the traditional blue. I was very worried about *Aziz* out on the wild sea alone. As usual in my dreams, I was aware of my real situation and had no escape from it.

Wind and sea moderated the next day, and by evening I had full main and No. 2 jib up. I didn't do much apart from reading but spent the afternoon listening to the finals of the Women's Singles at the Wimbledon Tennis Championships. It was a very exciting match in which the young Australian Evonne Goolagong just beat Margaret Smith. The radio was working well in spite of having hit the floor with a hideous crash the previous day.

About 11:30 that night, the log reached 2,000 miles. It had taken 20½ days. The first thousand had taken 10 days, so my speed through the water was about the same. The speed over the ground was unfortunately less as I had done a lot of tacking. I worked out that I had done 1,500 miles along my planned route and had another 2,000 to go. At this rate of progress it would take me another four weeks, which was longer than I had hoped.

The next day was Saturday, July 3. I had been at sea for three weeks. I hadn't spoken to anyone. I was getting worried that I would never get a message to anyone and would eventually turn up in America completely out of the blue.

About 1:30, I popped my head out of the cabin and there was a ship. She was abeam of me and traveling in the same direction. Out comes the lamp, and I signal AA AA AA, the call-up signal. No reply. I try again. No answer. I start sending *K K K*, thinking that perhaps they have mislaid their signal lamp. Now she is across my bow, about a mile away. "Please answer." I keep sending, but there is no response and gradually my excitement dies. I shake my fist at her and retire below in a huff to listen to tennis on the radio. Doesn't anyone keep a lookout?

I sit on the settee berth, light a cigarette, and plug in the earphones. The match is fascinating, and I am totally absorbed in it. Then "Hoot! Hoot!" A ship's foghorn.

I leap into the cockpit, and there is my ship, about a hundred yards away on the port quarter, moving at the same speed as I am. I wave, then dive below for the loudhailer. I can see a number of people waving, and I wave back, grinning all over my face like a Cheshire cat.

I think the captain wants me to slow down, but I don't do so as I think it is much safer if we both have maneuvering speed. He closes in. I nearly run under his bows but sheer off in time. Now we are about 50 feet apart.

I ask him to report me to London. He says he will,

in a good British accent, so I believe him. Then I ask for my position, and he tells me that we are at 37°48′N, 33°37′W. I tell him that I am on my way to America and that I am single-handed. He doesn't seem surprised, but asks if I need anything. I say, "No, thank you. Thank you very much for stopping by," and wave goodby.

As he draws ahead of me, I can see that he is the *Port Melbourne* from London, so I feel confident that the message will get through.

It would certainly simplify things if the new International Code of Signals had an equivalent to the old MIK signal which meant, "Please report me to Lloyds of London." There would then be no need to stop a ship just to report one's existence. I am very grateful to the captain of the *Port Melbourne*, for it must have cost him time and money slowing down his engines and then getting up speed again.

I felt delighted that my parents and friends would know that I was still alive. It cheered me up a lot to talk to someone; three weeks is a long time to be totally alone.

As soon as the ship left me, it was time to take a noon sight. It gave a latitude of 37°51′N, only three miles different from the latitude given me. Not bad at all. It might have been he that was out. My latitude, brought forward from the morning sight, is only 10 miles out. Not bad either. It is nice to know that my navigation is only miles out and not degrees.

# NINE

# Talking to Myself

ALTHOUGH WE were going along at a great lick under genoa and main, I soon changed down to the No. 1 jib, wondering what was coming, for there was a windy sky strewn with clouds from the southwest horizon. However, the wind died away, and by dusk I was heading south with a very light wind although the sky portended more vigorous conditions.

I stayed with the No. 1 jib all through the night, and eventually the wind arrived, rather more than I had bargained for, with two vicious squalls with heavy rain during the early hours. Then the wind died away completely. Dawn was ominous, a great red ball rising under high dark clouds with orange reflections on them. The sea was very slight and, as a breeze picked up from the south-southwest, we moved very easily. "If one could sail on a sea of mercury which did not ripple, one could go like the clappers even in a storm, as it is sea and not wind which stops a boat. . . . I think I will take up high-performance dinghy sailing on reservoirs!"

By midday the wind was quite strong, Force 5 or 6, and the sea had risen. There were plenty of white horses, and occasionally a wave would break over the side and into the cockpit. I had reduced sail to No. 2 jib and three reefs in the main, and we were still going along pretty fast. Before reefing I reckoned I was doing 7 knots at times, which was very exciting. *Aziz* pitched and rolled, and I had a job keeping steady enough to get a decent sight at noon.

During the afternoon the wind veered through 40°, and I was heading about west northwest, about 70° off the wind at a speed of 5½ knots. When I tried to get closer to the wind, there was a terrible pounding as *Aziz* tried to cope with a spiky sea, caused apparently by swells from two directions. Once I was caught standing in the cabin and not holding on and suddenly found myself hurled against the side. I hit my head on one of the bolts round the windows and caught my knee a terrific crack against the table.

There was a tremendous noise from *Aziz* pounding on the waves, things rattling around, the rigging creaking, and the water rushing past. I could not listen to the radio unless I lay in my bunk because the radio was behind my pillow so that it wouldn't slide to the floor. As it was Sunday, I had a hymn-singing session instead, and went through a considerable repertoire. I found that it made me quite tearful and gulpy, and I could hardly get through the sailors' hymn "Eternal Father." However, it was good for morale except that I found that I was singing out of tune.

It upset me to be out of tune as I have always had good pitch. I used to do a lot of choral singing at school and the university, which I enjoyed, and I was worried that my vocal chords might have atrophied. I wondered if I was, in fact, talking to myself. I hadn't been aware of doing so, but I was certainly thinking very loudly. I decided that I wasn't actually speaking when I found that I could think just as loudly while eating at the same time. About the only things I did say aloud were short, sharp expletives when something went awry. My voice sounded quite strange.

The singing that day set me off thinking about my university days. I started in Bristol in 1961 studying physics, the subject I had always liked best at school. Alas, when I reached university level I was completely out of my depth because it was so mathematical. I had been reasonably good at math at school but was totally bewildered by the lectures I was now attending. Admittedly this was not due wholly to an innate lack of understanding but also to the distracting influence of first love. Anyway, I failed all my exams at the end of the first year.

The authorities were kind and allowed me to stay, but I had to find a new subsidiary subject to replace applied math. I selected psychology. I knew nothing about it but thought it might be interesting to find out. I took to it immediately. I was particularly interested in how people perceive the physical world. I also enjoyed ethology, the study of the behavior of animals in their natural environment, but I never had much sympathy with the rats-in-cages type of animal psychology, and none at all with the physiological psychologists who maim animals to satisfy their curiosity.

Because of my mechanical bent I went into applied experimental psychology when I graduated. I enjoyed the work very much although it involved little of the layman's "psychology": personality studies, psychoanalysis, group psychology, and so on. Originally I took a very mechanical approach to the human being, concerned only with what goes in, and what comes out in response, and not in what goes on inside. Now I realize that personal and social factors are supremely important in determining how an individual will react. It is no wonder that psychology is still a disorganized body of knowledge. Predicting an individual's behavior is like trying to predict what a single molecule is going to do, but vastly more complex because all the individual's past experience will affect his reaction.

I have spent all my working life doing research of one kind or another. I now realized that the things I enjoyed most have been the craftsman's side of the job, not the academic side. I like the art of designing experiments so that the results will be informative. I like designing and building apparatus. I like doing statistical analysis, which is a craft and not a science.

Having detached myself from the academic world, with its posing and pretensions. I could see that I do not really have a scientific mind. While I am fascinated by ideas, I am more interested in personal than "objective" truth. I adore intelligent discussion for its own sake, for the pleasure I get from striking sparks between my mind and others'. I do not have the singlemindedness to concentrate on a small aspect of knowledge as a scientist must.

*Aziz* bucketed through the night while I slept. By morning the wind had increased to a hearty Force 6, so I changed from the No. 2 jib to the No. 3. This change did not seem to make much difference to our headlong flight, so I took off the No. 3 and we ambled along at about two knots. The No. 2 was old and baggy and the No. 3 was new and shapely, so I suppose they were giving about the same amount of lift despite the difference in area. There would have been more drag from the No. 2. From now on I rarely used it for windward work.

It was much more comfortable with no headsail, and I was particularly pleased because my bunk no longer got dollops of spray on it. I modified my jib, changing technique for heavy weather so that I didn't have to go on the foredeck while *Aziz* was in full flight. It was very difficult to work on because of the jerky motion and the solid water pouring over me. Now I got the jib down and lashed to the rails before taking the sail bags forward, and similarly removed the bags before hoisting the new sail. This needed more stages but was probably no more time-consuming since I could work more efficiently.

Now that we were almost hove to, I could hear the waves breaking. They sounded like a heavy sigh—Ssssshhh—and I noticed that the ones that hit the boat were usually not audible, only the ones that passed astern. I wondered what it would be like in really heavy seas such as those in the Southern Ocean. I could imagine them coming like an express train to crash hideously over the decks.

We had logged 128 miles in the 24 hours to 1000 hours, at an average of 5⅓ knots, which was not bad going, and most of it in the right direction. The noon-to-noon run by sights—that is, in a straight line—was 106 miles. I was pleased to have done so well despite the weather.

During the afternoon the wind veered gradually through 90° and eased a little, and at 1900 hours the barometer started to rise, so I raised the No. 3 jib. An hour later I unreefed to the first batten, and by midnight I had full main and No. 1 jib and was going nicely in a Force 2–3 northwesterly.

At 0100 hours I could see dark clouds ahead and shortly after there was a brief squall with a rush of wind, followed by a calm during which I dropped the mainsail because the boom was thrashing from side to side as *Aziz* rolled. After a while the wind started to rise again, and with it the sea; by the next afternoon we were back to a Force 5–6 from the northeast, after which it dropped a little and carried on veering.

By midnight we were almost on a dead run with a Force 3 wind, so I took down the main and hoisted the No. 1 jib as a twin for the No. 2. It turned out to be a real battle, for, as I hauled up the sail with wind still coming from astern, it flew forward pulling out the whole length of the sheet. Then it blew across to the wrong side, dragging the sheet under the bows. *Aziz* promptly sailed over it, and the sheet became wrapped round the rudder.

I got out a spinnaker sheet, clipped it on to the errant jib, and the same thing nearly happened again. I managed to tame the beast and get the sail drawing. Then I unclipped the original sheet, untied the knot in the cockpit end and hauled it in. Luckily it did not jam between the rudder and the hull, for that would have created serious problems. I don't know how I would have got it free. I might have had to go over the side and try to pull it loose.

Having sorted that out, I tried to put a pole on the No. 1 to keep it spread out. The wind was too strong for me, and I couldn't get the inner end hooked on to the mast. This requires brute strength as I hadn't fitted any uphauls, downhauls, or outhauls to my poles.

Next morning, Day 26, I found two flying fish on deck, each about one inch long. "It is like magic, these things happening to me, when I have read about them happening to the heroes."

I also found a messy lump of oil on the foredeck, which was a nasty surprise. I hadn't seen any signs of it floating about, but I suppose that most bits are too small to be easily visible. The water was very clean and clear, and there were no signs of the pollution that people had predicted I would find.

I took sights in the morning and at noon and fixed my position as 37°39′N, 41°13′W. This was Day 26. At last I could change charts from one showing Europe and the Atlantic to one showing the Atlantic and America.

"Hooray! It is nice to have my destination on the chart instead of my starting point."

# TEN

# Scare

I WAS STANDING in the cockpit idly viewing the panorama of blue sky and sea when out of the corner of my eye I saw a brown splotch floating past. It looked like seaweed but was gone before I could tell. Then I saw another splotch approaching, and sure enough it was weed. It was yellow ocher in color and appeared to consist of small bladders attached to one another by raffia. I was very surprised to see it there, for I thought it was the type of weed found in the Sargasso Sea, well away to the southwest. I could only assume that it had drifted up in the Gulf Stream, being unwilling to suppose that my navigation was that far out.

I assumed that these few pieces were around just by chance, but I soon discovered that the whole ocean was scattered with such bits of weed. I got used to having to clear it off the log line and saw it every day until I was the other side of the Gulf Stream. I wanted to catch a piece in the bucket to see whether there was any marine life attached to it, for I had read stories of little crabs and miniature monsters living in floating weed. However, I didn't dare risk my only bucket in such a venture, so I never found out if the stories were true. The pieces cut from the log line were deserted as one would expect, for spinning round and round is not a natural mode of life for any creature.

That afternoon I discovered a minor tragedy. I was poking around the forward cabin searching for the container of Ryvita packets when I noticed that the lower stowage on the starboard side had about three inches of evil-looking browny orange liquid in it. It turned out to be a mixture of kerosene and orange juice. I assumed that the kerosene had been lurking somewhere since the original spillage, for since then I had kept the containers in the cockpit. The orange juice came from a plastic bottle which had cracked at the edge of a dent.

The tragedy was that this unappetizing liquid had found its way into the large square tin containing a considerable quantity of fruit cake and parkin my mother had baked for me. Fortunately she had wrapped everything in aluminum foil so the penetration was limited, but I had to cut off the outside layer of each cake. The parkin was easy to remedy for it had changed color where it was wet, but the fruit cake was difficult as it was rich and damp to start with.

To cap my anger at this despoiling of my goodies, I managed to cover the cockpit with crumbs and mixed fruit by misjudging my throw when jettisoning the soggy bits. I sat down and sulked.

Next morning I was sleeping peacefully when I was suddenly brought to consciousness by a thump above my head, immediately followed by a lot of fluttering. I thought that a whole flight of flying fish must have come aboard; I lay there for a few moments listening to the fluttering and anticipating fresh fish. Then I dragged myself out of the bunk and climbed into the cockpit.

One solitary flying fish lay on the seat, fluttering his fins spasmodically. He had a bloody nose, and I guessed that he had flown into the side of the cockpit. I tried to pick it up so that I could hit it on the head and kill it quickly, but it flapped so much that I couldn't get hold of it. After a few rather tentative tries, I gave up and left it to suffocate. I went back to bed thinking that when I got up it would be dead, and I could eat it for breakfast.

I felt cowardly leaving it there to die slowly, for it brought to mind one of the times when I really despised myself. I was driving near Salisbury Plain when a game bird of some sort leaped out of the hedge into my windshield. A mess of red and yellow fluid blotted out my vision, but I felt the lump hit the roof before bouncing off. It went in a high arc, and I watched it through the rear-view mirror as it dropped to the road behind me, a whirling mess of feathers.

I felt obliged to go back to see whether it was still alive, but couldn't force myself to, in case it was. I drove on feeling like a real worm. I should have gone back and hoped that if it happened again I would. I am sure that familiarity with such situations enables one to control one's responses and act in a more reasonable way. I don't like killing or hurting any living thing though I am sure I could learn to do so—for food or out of pity. I would hate to learn to kill for sport.

My flying fish was delicious fried in butter. I could have done with about three more. This one was the first I had seen of an edible size. It was about 7 inches long, silver below and navy blue above, with a blunt nose and, of course, the wings. These are really over-developed pectoral fins and act as gliding planes rather than true wings. When spread out the fish has a silhouette similar to a World War II Spitfire, the wings being quite broad and curved on the trailing edges. I never saw any real flying exhibitions but occasionally saw small fish skitter upwind when frightened by *Aziz* pounding up on them.

Luck was with me that morning. When I went out to fetch in my breakfast, I noticed that the topping lift, a line from the end of the boom to the masthead and down to the base of the mast, had come unshackled from the boom. The two ends of the lift were wrapped round the port shrouds, fortunately within my reach—

if they had not been I would have had to do some
acrobatics to get them down. The shackle which had
come undone was stainless steel and I replaced it with
a large, bronze one. I hadn't wired the pin of the stainless one, which I should have done. Unlike bronze and
galvanized shackles, stainless ones do not corrode and
jam solid.

I looked over the side and found that some large
fish were swimming under the boat. At first I thought
they were dolphins, but they weren't. There were five
of them, each about 4 feet long and with the character-
istic side fins of the shark family. I noticed them just
after I had cleaned out the flying fish over the side. I
made sure that I didn't let my hands hang over in case
these fish might fancy a taste of my blood.

They stayed with me at least till lunchtime, when
a breeze ruffled the water and I could no longer see
them. They didn't do very well out of me, for the only
scraps I offered them were the bones of my fish.

I spent a domestic afternoon, washing everything I
could lay my hands on: dishes, clothes, my hair, myself.
It was a perfect drying day, sunny and breezy, and
despite being washed in salt water the clothes dried
pretty well. My hair felt a lot better, a change from
the nasty sticky rats' tails it usually was. It was then
about shoulder-length, and I was tempted at times to
cut it short so that it wouldn't get tangled and would
keep out of my eyes. But vanity always won. I had been
growing it for about two years, and it was just reaching
a reasonable length, as it grew very slowly. I knew that

if I cut it off in a fit of pique I would regret it later, so I put up with the nasty sticky string that it turned into whenever the weather was bad.

During the afternoon I saw a tanker quite close, about a mile away. I signaled to him but got no reply as he steamed on toward Europe. I was not so distressed this time, having passed a message a few days earlier. It is quite probable that he saw me but did not reply because of the trouble it would take. I could not blame him for this, for I was not sending distress signals, which he would have been obliged to respond to. Still, it would have been nice of him to stop.

I worked out an arrival date based on my average progress so far. It came to 16 days hence, which was July 24. That would be 42 days altogether, the time I had estimated it would take. So I was up to schedule so far.

I was rather sorry to think that the voyage was more than half over. I had really settled down to the life and could hardly imagine anything different. I could understand now how the real long-distance boys had endured being alone for so long. I was able to fill my days quite happily and no longer thought much about others. I felt detached from the world of people. Although the radio kept me well informed, I did not feel concerned about current affairs.

I found that I was also detached from time. Dates were merely names to identify days with and not markers of the passage of time. When I heard on the radio that some event was due to take place in August, I would think, "But why are they telling us that, it is a long time away."

Associated with this feeling of being stationary in time was a feeling of being stationary in space. When I looked at the eastern horizon, I did not really believe that there was all that sea there and that I had crossed it. I felt that I was in the same place, with the sea moving past me; there was no sense of progressing.

The evening brought a sweet-and-sour experience. Shortly before dusk I signaled a ship heading west. She flashed back immediately, which impressed me. Then she altered course toward me, and although she slowed down, she was still moving quite fast as she overtook me to leeward and crossed my bows. I was afraid that she would carry on without letting me pass a message. But she stopped dead about half a mile ahead and lay there, wallowing.

It took me quite some time to sail up to her, for the wind was light, and like a fool I aimed to go up the windward side. At the last moment I realized that this was not a very good idea as I might easily run out of maneuvering space. I sailed around her stern, a peculiar affair with great gates, and saw her name: *Lash Turkiye* of New York. I sailed up her starboard side and hailed them through the loudhailer. I got a reply but could not see where it came from. However, I requested that he report me to Lloyds of London, and he said he would. I explained that I was single-handed to Newport, Rhode Island, and he asked me if I wanted anything. I said no, thank you, and thanks for stopping, and as I had by now almost overtaken him, I waved goodby and put back on my course.

It was now getting dark, and we both had our navigation lights on. I kept a close watch on the ship and noticed that she remained stationary for a while and then started moving off on her original course. Now it was quite dark, and I could only see her lights. Suddenly I noticed that the pattern of lights was changing. Now I could see both red and green lights, and that meant she was heading straight for me. I waited for her to swing round but she didn't.

"Hellfire, she's coming straight for me." I got out the torch and shone it from the cockpit to supplement my white stern light, thinking that perhaps she hadn't realized where I was. Still she kept on coming. I started to sweat. Her lights got closer. I flashed her with the signal lamp and she replied immediately. Alas, I cannot read Morse and didn't know what she meant. At least she knew that I was there. But still she came on and now her lights were looming over me. I hastily unhitched the self-steering and swung *Aziz* around until I was heading back toward England!

She got the message then and turned back on to her course and soon her lights vanished over the horizon. I expect she wondered what I was playing at. I certainly couldn't work out what she was up to. I was very grateful to her for stopping but did "go off" big ships for a while.

## ELEVEN

# A Visitor

THE NEXT morning I got out the *Admiralty Pilot for the East Coast of America*. If anyone is looking for horror stories, let him invest in an *Admiralty Pilot*. For sheer matter-of-fact spine-chilling comment, there is nothing to beat them. Remarks like "small ships have been known to founder under such conditions" become quite horrifying when one realizes that their idea of a small ship is something about 200 feet long. One of my favorite parts concerns a narrow passage between two islands. It warns the helmsman to keep a steady course, for, if he does not, he will be "swept on to the rocks to almost certain destruction."

## A Visitor

The *Pilot for America* made pretty nasty reading, particularly when describing the weather. Apparently there is a corridor just off the coast up which depressions rush, one after the other, bringing rapid changes in conditions. There is a small chance of hurricanes during July and a much greater chance during August. There is also a very high probability of encountering fog, an unattractive prospect.

For comparison I read the *West Coast of England Pilot*. That sounded pretty horrifying, too, so I was a little consoled, knowing that the weather there is frequently very pleasant.

I acquired an escort: three pilot fish. At least, I assumed they were pilot fish as they had very marked stripes. These went round the body instead of along it, and they looked as though they were wearing football jerseys. They were very curious and would rush out from beneath *Aziz* to examine every bit of rubbish I threw over. I didn't try to catch them as I had become disillusioned about my skill as a fisherman. Besides, it would have been inhospitable. I am not sure that they were pilot fish; somehow they looked too vulgar to fit my image.

The next day, July 10, Day 29, was still quiet with little wind. I took advantage of the dry decks to fiberglass the forehatch lid, which was crumbling at the edges. It was poorly designed, as the circular lid was held down only by a lashing to an eye in the center of the lid. It was consequently deformed, allowing water to penetrate under the edges. I made a rather crude repair by putting fiber-glass matting over the faulty patches and soaking it with resin. The resin set so quickly after the hardener was added that I hardly had time to transfer it from the pot to the repair before it went tacky. I suppose the temperature was too high. However, the result, if not beautiful, looked strong. I also bolted an eye to the inside of the cabin roof so that I could hang the Tilley lamp up.

I was having a well-deserved rest, reading a fascinating book about children growing up, and placidly crunching a clear mint, when I realized that my mouth felt strange. I poked about with my tongue and discovered that a large chunk had disappeared from my left upper back tooth. Getting out my powder compact, I squinted in the tiny mirror, dragging my lip back to see what the extent of the damage was. As far as I could tell, the filling in the tooth was still intact, and the break was not under the gum, so it was not as vast a rock fall as I had thought.

It didn't hurt, which was a good thing since I hadn't any Novocain with me. I had had a hole in that tooth for years before having it filled specially for this voyage and had never had any pain from it, so I was hopeful that I wouldn't suffer now. It would be unheroic to give up the venture because of a toothache.

I was up several times during the night for a strong breeze had come up. I nursed *Aziz* through a few squalls, and after one of these sorties out on deck, I switched on the radio and discovered that reception was superb. I picked up domestic stations from Europe on the medium and longwave bands, listened to Late Night Extra on

BBC 2, and was able to hear the 0030 (BST) shipping forecast for British waters, which was interesting. They said that there was a ridge of high pressure from the Azores to the western approaches to the Channel, which agreed with what I had surmised. It was nice to hear the familiar style of the domestic BBC. I was then about 2,300 miles from the transmitter.

The following morning I saw a polythene bag floating past and thought it was a sign of the pollution we hear so much about. It wasn't. On closer inspection this bag turned out to be a Portuguese Man o' War, a fascinating and deadly creature. It looks rather like a jellyfish with a "sail" running diagonally across its back and has long tendrils hanging down. These are extremely poisonous. It is not, in fact, a single animal but is a colony of several hundreds of individuals living an interdependent existence. This one was out of bounds, for they usually stay within the trade wind belts nearer the equator.

A little later I had a visitor, an elegant tern who headed straight for the boat. He seemed tired and tried to make a landing on the masthead. This was a real comedy act. He would fly downwind, swing around, and make a run upwind, looking like an aircraft on a bombing run. As he approached *Aziz*, up would go his wings, down would come his feet and—oops! the masthead would whip away from his hopeful feet and off he would go for another try.

After five or six goes, he gave up and flew around looking rather forlorn. I hoped he would land on the deck, but he didn't even try—too shy, I suppose. After about 20 minutes, he veered off and flew away to the south. I hope he knew that there was no land that way for thousands of miles.

That evening I had an elegant cocktail hour. I dressed up in a mini dress, put on makeup, brushed my hair free of tangles, and doused myself with perfume. I felt gorgeous! I had acquired a splendid all-over tan, but had difficulty in finding how dark it was since I was without the normal bikini marks. Eventually I found two white stripes under the rings I always wear, one on each hand. These rings were both presents, and I would look at them and think about the donors. This would bring back memories of good times afloat and ashore, like scenes remembered from a film.

The next day was July 12. I had been at sea for a month. I was surprised how quickly the previous 10 days had passed, and I hoped that the next 10 days would go as quickly. Yet I had no feeling of covering distance. It was as if I was the center of the world; all things were relative to me. I could see no boundary to the ocean, and my chart was folded so that no land appeared on it. I was the only person in my world.

The barometer started to fall in the afternoon, and the wind rose from the south southwest to a healthy Force 4–5. We were screaming along at 6½ knots with the genoa set, but the self-steering was not happy and I changed down to the No. 2 jib. There were a number of squalls which brought brief increases in wind speed. They were like angry cats spitting and hissing as they scampered across the sky.

*Aziz* kept falling off waves, a most unpleasant sensation. There is the suspense as you become weightless and then a hideous crash as the bows smite the water. I had to nurse her through some of the squalls and was very cross with one that sprayed salt water into my cup of lemon tea, making it completely undrinkable.

The wind increased in the night, and I was roused out to put three reefs in the main. I wrote in the navigation log "previously going like a runaway racehorse," so it must have been wild. I was not prone to writing such comments in the log—usually I stuck to factual information.

At dawn I put on the storm jib, and three hours later I hove to on the port tack. The wind was now Force 6–7, still from the southwest. The seas were not particularly high, perhaps 10 or 12 feet, but steep enough to be uncomfortable. Not many broke over *Aziz* although the bows dipped beneath the crests at times.

Shortly after heaving to, there was torrential rain with strong gusts of wind. That was the final fling. The sky brightened, the rain stopped, and the wind veered and eased. Soon *Aziz* was moving again with a northeasterly Force 4.

I was glad the squalls had gone away, for I found them frightening. There would be a sudden burst of wind and torrential rain which blotted out the horizon and reduced my world to a few square yards of steaming, surging, steely water. My inexperience worried me, for I could only guess how I should handle the boat and whether I was asking too much of her.

I had dropped myself in at the deep end, undertaking this trip, and was forced to learn quickly about sailing and fear. I am not infinitely brave, as some people would have me. There was no place for bravery out there, for bravery is the willful acceptance of a challenge. It is a reaction to pride and fear. Without fear there is no challenge: without bravery no need to accept the challenge. Yes, it was brave to set out, but now there was no choice. I could not refuse the challenge when life itself was the prize.

But would there be a limit to the amount of fear I could stand? Would fear—fear of death—finally break the unity of mind, body, and reality which is sanity?

I had to face reality and accept the fears and the joys and the boredom. I could not weaken.

TWELVE

# Bad Weather Coming

I MADE GOOD progress in spite of the squalls and discovered that I had achieved an average speed of over 5 knots in the 24 hours up to 1830 hours. This was gratifying and compensated for the discomfort involved. The temperature had dropped quite noticeably, so I went back to wearing trousers, a little sadly, for I guessed that this was the end of my Garden of Eden sailing.

I had spent much of the previous weeks in a state of undress. The skin is a comfortable and practical covering: it dries quickly when wet, is easy to keep clean, and is cool in the heat of the day. Often when I had to

135

change a foresail I would undress rather than put on my oilskins, to save getting anything wet. The only disadvantage of this was that I had to kneel on the foredeck, which had a rough surface. This was decidedly uncomfortable at first, but after a while the skin on my knees and the top of my feet hardened up.

The main disadvantage of skin is that it is not very resistant to abrasion. I had become sufficiently at one with *Aziz* to avoid many severe collisions with her, but I was frequently bruised for that is unavoidable. My legs had a magnificent display of purple, blue, yellow, and brown splotches—my substitute for modern art.

I enjoyed the freedom of nakedness and became unaware of it as an unusual mode of dress. I was caught out on one occasion. I sighted a ship on the horizon and leaped out into the cockpit to wave. Then I hurriedly leaped back into the cabin to cover myself. Fortunately they were too far away to have enjoyed the mid-ocean follies!

I was eagerly looking forward to meeting Americans on their home ground and discovering more of what America really is. Through our news media in England we get an odd view of an America full of hippies, rioting students and Negroes and prisoners, snatch thieves, murderers, corrupt police, bodies lying ignored in the streets, drug takers, and pushers, striking workers, and a huge materialistic, unthinking, overfriendly mass of once-divorced middle-class vegetables. And, of course, magnificent scenery.

I wouldn't be surprised if Americans have similar

views of Europe, though perhaps they are more char-
itable. I think there is a great envy of America in Europe,
as well as a certain feeling of being more civilized—
sour grapes, perhaps.

The following day was a workday. I cleared up a
fair bit of the untidiness that had started to offend my
eye. At last I cleaned out the sawdust and wood shavings
that were remnants of Brian's strengthening of the bulkhead. I had neglected this job because it involved taking
the gas burner off its gimbals, the bearings which allow
it to swing. This was not particularly difficult, requiring
only a bit of levering with a screwdriver, but it was inclined to be mucky as the black grease from the bearings
always managed to spread itself over me.

That job done, I set to work on the boltheads which
protruded through the cabin roof. First I filed them
down so that they were fairly smooth and then arduously
rubbed off the rust marks on the surrounding fiber glass.
Then I rubbed off the rust marks on the cockpit sides
where the washers on the bolts taking the tiller line
blocks had rusted so badly that I suspected that they
were not stainless as they should have been.

While I was doing this, I leaned on the lower starboard lifeline which promptly broke. It had rusted
through in secret with no external sign of decay. I replaced it with a length of green line which was just long
enough to enable me to tie a knot in the end. Finally I
pumped the bilge, which had about 6 inches of water
in it.

I took a sight in the morning which put me further

west than was likely. According to my noon positions that day and the day before I had covered 158 miles—a likely story. That would be an average of 6½ knots. My noon-to-noon run on the log was only 114 miles. Much more probable, considering that the wind was quite light. Only on later analysis did I realize how bad these fixes were.

The wind veered and increased during the afternoon, and by evening it was a boisterous Force 4 from just west of south. I shortened sail to No. 3 jib and a single reef in the mainsail. The barometer was falling steadily, and I was afraid that more rough stuff was on the way.

I spent the evening reading *Cancer Ward* by Solzhenitsyn. Despite its being about pretty depressing conditions in Russia I enjoyed it, for it is written with humor and sensibility. I had nearly left it behind when someone told me that it was very depressing but was glad I hadn't.

During the night I got up to put another two reefs in the main. We still carried on at a good speed and were fairly comfortable as the sea was not very disturbed.

"However, I must say that I am getting tired of the constant motion, and my thoughts turn more and more to the end of the voyage. I find that I am more apprehensive now, which is odd as one would expect to gain rather than lose confidence. I think that the trouble is that I am worrying more about arriving safely and in the right place."

What I meant was that earlier in the voyage I had not considered a future different from the present, a time when I would no longer be at sea. Now I started to think of life ashore, a life of physical comfort, which made me dissatisfied with the discomfort I was experiencing now.

The following day, Day 35, started well with *Aziz* making good progress on the right course for America. However, during the afternoon the wind rose quickly to Force 5 and kept on rising until by midnight it was Force 7–8. We were thrashing along in a horrifying way. My nerves could not stand the frequent crashes as *Aziz* smashed her bows on to the waves, for I was afraid that something would break, leaving me a long way from safety. So I took off the jib, and we waddled along at about 2 knots, with the main reefed to the second batten. It had stretched quite a lot and looked like a baggy handkerchief. I could not reef further than the second batten because the boom dropped so low that it touched the lifelines. Had it been really necessary, I would have had to roll a cushion in the sail to lift the boom.

The morning sea was like blue-black ink, with an occasional fleck of green as the light shone through a breaking wave. The air was a little warmer, so I was back to sail-changing in the nude, apart from the harness.

As I was running short of reading matter, I got out my complete works of Shakespeare. I have always found it hard work reading the plays. I suppose this is due to the significance that had been invested in them by generations of critics, making it difficult to take the plays at face value and enjoy the flow of words and action. I keep stopping dead when the language is obscure. By the time I have made sense of it, I have forgotten what was going on. The historical ones are the worst, so I decided to pick an easy play. I lighted on *The Tempest*. It was a peculiarly appropriate choice, but the joke didn't dawn on me until after my arrival in America.

## THIRTEEN

# Trouble

IT WAS A rough night. At 0130 hours I thought the wind had moderated a touch, and raised the No. 3 jib. Then I went into a troubled sleep, bumping against the sides of the bunk and being awakened by dollops of water falling on my head. It seemed to get rougher and rougher. After a couple of hours I could no longer stand the crashing and jerking and reluctantly climbed out of my nest and dressed in oilskins.

I went into the cockpit and headed *Aziz* away from the wind. This eased the motion some, but after two hours it was as bad as ever, so once again I climbed out.

I took down the jib and left the boat moving slowly to windward. It was a pitch-black night, but lightning flashed now and then, showing banks of high, dark cumulus. Several squalls rushed by, accompanied by torrential rain, as though someone had turned on a huge shower at full pressure, and gusts of wind whistled through the rigging.

I was putting in the top washboard to keep out the rain. I turned the wooden latch and—ouch!—squashed the middle finger of my right hand. It hurt like fury for a couple of minutes, and I froze where I was, clutching my finger and letting the pain wash over me. Then it eased and became bearable. The nail was badly bruised, but I hoped it would not come off. This was my most painful injury to date. I supposed I had got off lightly.

I didn't feel like sleeping after that, so I switched on the radio. I picked up several local American stations on the medium band. It was fun listening except that they seemed to be obsessed by baseball, which I did not understand at all. The reports seemed to be totally composed of jargon words which meant absolutely nothing to me, although it was all clearly of vital significance to the broadcasters. I could sympathize with American visitors to Britain during the cricket season, who listen to the conversation with a bemused, rather condescending expression as though they pity the natives who still believe in magic rites.

At 0930 hours I raised the jib again and survived a couple of squalls, and then there was a terrific wind veer through 90°. This pleased me since it meant that I could steer a course to take me a little further south. I was worried that the almost incessant southwesterlies would push me north into the main current of the Gulf Stream. I wanted to avoid this until I was closer to America.

It was clear that I was now in the Gulf Stream and out of the rather arid sea I had been crossing, for the phosphorescence of the water at night had increased enormously. It was a different sort of phosphorescence from that I had encountered on the way to the Azores. There it was fine-grained, a comet's tail behind the boat. Here it was a lot of quite large bright lights like glow-worms, giving a spectacular burst of light as the bows crashed down and flung out a sheet of cold fire. I could watch it for hours as it formed new and ever-changing galaxies and nebulae, a visible cosmos to replace the one hidden by the overcast.

I got out Adlard Coles' *Heavy Weather Sailing,* which contains descriptions of some particularly bad gales and hurricanes, with discussion about the tactics used in them. It has some horrifying pictures of waves. They frightened me so much that I hurriedly hid the book away. I must have been close to the position where Humphrey Barton had his famous knockdown in *Vertue* *XXXV* when crossing to America. A huge wave flung the boat on to her beam ends, the doghouse smashed in, and a peaceful meal was turned into a chaos of swirling water. Quick thinking and excellent seamanship saved them.

I had a minor frustration during the morning when

trying to take a bath. I selected a suitably wet-looking squall, undressed, and stood under its shower covering myself with liquid detergent. I had just got myself nicely soaped and was about to rinse off when the rain stopped. There I was covered with sticky slime. I tried to wipe it off with paper towels without much success. Fortunately another squall arrived fairly soon, and I was able to rinse off. I felt nice and clean—a pleasant change from the stickiness of sea water.

I began to recognize the pattern of weather. It was roughly as follows:

Rain, gradually increasing in intensity, followed by wind, gradually increasing.

Then, suddenly, torrential rain and high wind which veers sharply. The sea is completely subdued and looks like steaming, rolling hills. Visibility is 50 yards or so.

Gradually the sky lightens and the wind eases, followed by the rain. The wind drops completely, and the boat rolls horribly in a flat calm, the boom thrashing from side to side.

After a little the wind comes up again, usually from its original direction.

The whole process lasts 10 to 25 minutes. "I am getting a bit blasé about these occurrences now, though I still get up and watch what is going on. It is going to be a bind if it is like this all the way across the Gulf Stream. However, it could be worse. Like a hurricane!"

I kept having to haul the log line in to remove weed from it. There was still plenty of weed about, and now it seemed to collect in tablecloth-size pieces instead of tea-tray or dinner-plate size. There was frequently some around the self-steering oar. I couldn't get it off easily, so would wait for it to come off of its own accord, as it always did. It didn't come off the log line, however, and when quite a bit collected it caused a terrific drag, as though we were towing a sea anchor.

The log was no longer working well, and I wondered if the strain had damaged the mechanism. The line no longer revolved gently all the time but would wait until it was fully wound up. Then it would whiz around at top speed for about half a minute before stopping to rewind itself. Perhaps it just needed oiling. I imagine I lost a few miles from the record because of this.

The day passed with a number of squalls. The sea was not particularly large, perhaps 8 feet. In the afternoon I was looking at the clouds when I saw a shiny, round gray object high above me. It seemed to be moving against the wind, but I guess that was an illusion. I couldn't imagine what it was. A flying saucer? I concluded that it must have been a meteorological balloon. It was funny seeing a manmade object up there.

In the evening I saw a small ship approaching. He seemed to be heading for me, so I went out and took over the steering. However he passed safely a few hundred yards astern. In spite of thinking he had seen me, I made no attempt to communicate as conditions were such that I didn't want to get close to him. Anyway, since the *Lash Turkiye* incident I had become wary of ships.

Had it been an emergency I would have tried to speak to him, but it would have been difficult to avoid one of us drifting down on the other with consequent damage to me. I wished again for an MIK signal.

That night I was finally forced out of the quarter berth as it had become too sodden for comfort. I moved on to the saloon berth. This had the disadvantage that I needed a leeboard when on the starboard tack to stop me arriving slowly or suddenly on the cabin floor. Instead of using the canvas leeboard, which was stowed under the mattress, I used the table, which bridges the berth. This proved quite satisfactory. I was much more comfortable now and happily ignored the water which fell where my head had been.

At 0100 hours the wind had increased to a steady Force 6, and I took the jib off, allowing *Aziz* to wallow along at about 1½ knots, about 60° off the wind. The sky was clear, and there was a spectacular display of lightning around the horizon. It was not close enough to be audible, which was a relief. I still had not gotten used to the idea of being the highest object in miles, just right for a lightning strike.

I slept well, despite the howling wind and rocking boat, and in the morning felt sufficiently confident to raise the No. 3 jib. I was fed up with the slow progress I had been making and thought that the wind had eased somewhat.

Alas, at 1020 hours I was hit by a terrific squall with what I described in the log as hurricane-force winds— certainly an exaggeration. But I should think that the gusts reached Force 9 and probably Force 10. *Aziz* was laid right over, and I scrambled into the cockpit to ease off the sheets, cursing the fact that I had become too casual about squalls. I looked forward and noticed a halyard tail flying horizontally from the mast. Hang on! —that's a funny place for a halyard to come from. I glanced over the rigging and realized with a groan that the port after lower shroud was not there.

I let go the sheets and *Aziz* stopped dead, lying broadside to the wind, the sails flapping and cracking. I rushed up to the mast, not stopping for safety harness, dropped the mainsail, and let go the jib halyard. I fought the jib into a bundle and stuffed it against the pulpit and lifelines. Then I hurried below to fetch the sail ties. I flipped one around the jib and then crudely bundled the mainsail on to the boom, quite a job as the boom was swinging wildly, its end frequently dipping into the seas. As soon as the sail was tied down I hauled the boom central. Then I went forward to look at the shroud.

It had broken at the bottom where the wire was round a metal thimble. A single strand had unwound from the top, suggesting that all was not well up there. I twisted the loose wire into the halyards to stop it swinging around and went below for a cigarette, a whisky, and a think.

Conditions were bad. The wind was a good Force 7, gusting 8 or 9, and the waves were very large—about 15 or 20 feet, I estimated, trying not to overstate things. The sea was a greeny gray with white icing, and the rigging was howling as the wind roared through it.

It was a piece of luck that the shroud had broken at the bottom. At least I wouldn't have to climb the mast with the boat rolling furiously. The bottom of the shroud had been attached to the rigging screw by a pin through a loop in the end of the wire. This loop was formed by taking the wire around a metal former and squeezing a metal sleeve over the two parts. The wire had broken at the base of the loop, so the sleeve was still left attached to the wire.

I decided that the best solution would be to take the wire round a block and lash it in position with thin terylene line. With luck, the sleeve would stop the end of the wire from pulling through the lashing. I would attach the block to the rigging screw with several turns of the same terylene line and then tighten up the screw to tension the shroud. I couldn't see any snags. When the boat was tossing about less violently I would try to get up the mast and put a rope on as an additional shroud.

I went out and completed the repair without any hitches. *Aziz* was pitching and rolling a lot, but not many waves were breaking over her. I tidied up the deck and went below to take stock of the situation.

Now that I had no immediate work to do, the shock of what had happened hit me. I was worried that conditions would get worse and that the rigging would not stand up. I imagined *Aziz* dismasted and washed by breaking waves.

I started to think about what would happen if I had to abandon ship. Even if I did attract the attention of a ship either by radio or by red distress flares, I did not see what she would do. How would they get me aboard, and what would happen to *Aziz*? It would be too rough to attempt to take her aboard, but they couldn't just leave her to float around, a menace to shipping. Perhaps they would deliberately run her down. I visualized the boat and all my possessions sinking through the quiet dark world to crumble under the pressure of water and lie on the bottom, a sad, twisted relic of a failure. Poor *Aziz*! And poor me!

But worse, suppose I had to take to the liferaft! How long could I survive if no one found me? It would take at least two months to drift back to Europe and that was rather too long, for even if my body survived I doubted that my mind would.

I started to think about death in a new way. Never before had I faced the prospect of imminent death, and I didn't like the idea. It may have been an unwarranted fear, but it was nonetheless real. Before I set out on this journey, I had felt that since one must die sometime, to die during an exploit like this would be a splendid way to go. I certainly didn't think that way now. I was upset by the thought of friendships lost—present and future. I felt it would be intolerable to die without having enjoyed what life has to offer. I thought now of the old people who, it is said, have nothing to live for. I could imagine the sadness of those who approach death still waiting to live. I did not fear the physical act of dying, but I did not want to be dead, for I have no certainty of a life after death, no feeling that there is something to look forward to.

I sat in the cabin feeling desolate.

# FOURTEEN

# Temptation Two

IT BLEW HARD all day, and the seas were like rocky mountains, large, jagged, and majestic. They seemed to have increased in size, and I presumed that the wind had been blowing over a considerable distance to have generated so large a sea. *Aziz* was lying ahull, pointing southeast and drifting slowly northeast.

I sat in the cabin smoking furiously, unable to concentrate on anything for more than a few minutes at a time. I wished I had never heard of sailing.

At last it seemed that the wind had eased, and at 2015 hours I raised the reefed mainsail. Twenty minutes later I took it down quickly as another burst of wind struck the boat. A couple of hours later the wind really had moderated, and I raised the main with its three reefs and hoisted the storm jib. *Aziz* seemed happy now, and we progressed well. While setting the jib, I was cheered to see a pretty blue fish with a yellow tail swimming just below the surface. It was about 3 feet long, and very active.

I hove to twice in the night when squalls arrived, for I was afraid that the shroud would not stand the strain. There was terrific lightning again, but it was quite a way off and I hoped that things were improving. I kept going steadily till noon the next day and thought the wind was dying away. There was still howling from the rigging, and I couldn't remember if it always howled and I hadn't noticed it earlier; I couldn't tell whether the wind was still strong. I found that I had lost confidence in my judgment of conditions. I was not certain how bad things really were. Looking back, however, I think my estimates were about right—if anything I was under-estimating.

In the morning I did so stupid a thing that I was tempted not to record it. I cut the log rotator adrift. What happened was that I had hauled in the line and found a particularly magnificent bundle of weed wrapped round it. After taking a photograph of it I started to pull it off by hand but it was rather tough so I got out my knife and started cutting the sea weed off. I was reckless in my knife work and instead of cutting the weed I sliced through the line. The whole lot fell overboard, log ro-

tator included. I blushed at my carelessness. I had no
spare, so from now on I would have to estimate my
speed. This meant that my dead reckoning of progress
would be even less accurate than before.

At noon I unrolled a reef from the main but soon I
had to roll it in again, for the wind started to rise again
and by mid-afternoon was back to Force 7. I took down
the main and kept going slowly with only the storm jib.

I was uncertain about my position, for I had not
been able to get a decent sight for a couple of days and
was not very sure of my rate and direction of drift when
lying ahull or sailing with very small sail area. However,
I was not close enough to the coast to be very worried,
and I knew that I must try to head about due west to
counteract the northeasterly set of the current. The Gulf
Stream current runs quite fast at its maximum—well
over 30 miles a day—but it is difficult to know where it is
running at that speed. I was hoping to cross the current
at right angles so as to get through as quickly as possible
and regretted that the bad weather made it so difficult to
hold a course. Moving so slowly meant that the current
had a greater effect on the direction made good.

I put up the main again that evening, and we
pounded along. Three hours later came a terrific slam
which threw bottles all over the place from a box on the
port forward berth. I promptly dropped the main before
clearing up the mess.

A jam jar had smashed in the well of cans, smearing
them with jam and broken glass. A bottle of disinfectant
had shattered into little pieces on the floor, the liquid

running into the bilge. The cabin smelled like a public restroom. I tried to clear up all the glass because I didn't want to cut my feet. I didn't pump the bilge as I rather enjoyed the new smell. At least, I thought, it will cover the smell of mildew and dirty clothes when I arrive in America.

"July 20, Day 39, 0100. I am sitting here with a brandy and orange juice cocktail and a cigarette, pretending that I am somewhere else than this particular corner of the Atlantic. I can just visualize myself in the Griffin at Dale with a bitter in one hand and a whiskey on the table and plenty of good company.

"I am beginning to think that these high winds are perpetual. If that is so, I am not sure what strategy to adopt. It might be better in the long run to go southeast out of the stream and then go west nearly to the coast before going north. But that would be a long way round, and if I can make even 40 miles a day directly I will do better. It may be that I am only making due north, in which case I shall wait until I am in the Labrador current and then tack down. I can't really abort to any other port as I don't have any detail charts for them.

"It might be quicker to go back to England!!"

The last remark was not entirely frivolous. I was tired of the continual struggle to make headway against the wind, and I was tired of being alone, of having to make decisions; but, most of all, I was frustrated that I couldn't approach the land which was so near. I knew I could reach Europe, but I had begun to doubt that I would ever reach America. If I could make only 40 miles a day toward America, which is against wind and current, I should be able to make 120 miles a day down wind and current.

I was tempted. It would solve the problem of how to get myself and *Aziz* back from America. But then I thought that no one would believe how close I had got. Anyway, I like to do what I have said I will do. I was damned if I would be called a failure having got so far. I could just hear the patronizing sympathy from the men. "Jolly good effort," they would say, adding mentally, "for a woman."

But the real reason I couldn't go back was that I knew that I couldn't live with my own cowardice. I am not brave enough to be a coward. You have to be very strong to do something cowardly and not despise yourself.

"It is as bad as ever today, if not worse. The sea is very confused, and the wind must be a Force 8.

"I think I shall go mad if it doesn't stop soon. I've already shed tears of frustration and depression and prayed for calm weather.

"Most of the time I just lie down and either read, listen to the radio or do nothing. It is very depressing and worrying."

I think I was in a state of mild shock. I sat for quite long periods in a daze, something I do not usually do.

That evening a squall came along, and with a vicious tug the jib sheet pulled the sheet lead out of the track. This is the block mounted on a slide that can be moved along a track down the side of the boat to alter the angle the sheet makes with the sail. The smaller the foresail, the further forward on the track must be the block. What had happened was that the eye holding the block to the slide had pulled out.

At first I thought of screwing an eye in the middle of the track as a compromise for all sheeting positions, but it was no good. I couldn't undo any of the screws holding the track down. I couldn't easily drill through the stainless steel track under the circumstances, and there wasn't sufficient width of wood under the track for me to screw into. I ended up by screwing the eye just aft of the track and making a chain of shackles from the base of the stanchion at the forward end of the track. I put a snap shackle on the sheet block so that I could easily transfer it from one position to the other. I used the shackle chain for the storm, No. 3, and No. 2 jibs, and the eye for the No. 1 jib and the genoa. It worked quite well, but the stanchion groaned horribly under the strain.

There was a lot of wind during the night, which I spent under storm jib alone. I didn't raise the main until 1300 hours the next day, by which time the wind had eased to Force 4–5, when I put on the No. 3 jib and took two reefs in the main.

I took a couple of sights, and the position they gave put me about 360 miles from Newport. This was encouraging, for if the weather remained decent I might be able to get there in four or five days. It was now July 21st, so I might be in on the 25th or 26th.

The barometer was the highest it had been for days, but the weather was erratic with a number of squalls interspersed with blue sky. The wind piped up again in the evening, and I put back the storm jib and put another reef in the main.

At midnight I hove to for the night. I had the best display of lightning yet, making the whole sky a curtain of vivid lilac. There was no moon, and I couldn't see when squalls were coming. This was a nuisance as I didn't carry much canvas lest I be caught unawares and have the shroud go again. There was plenty of rain, and I caught a bowlful, which tasted delicious.

In the morning the wind was down to Force 4–5, and I put on the No. 3 jib. We went along at a good speed, and I thought that we were getting on nicely toward America.

After lunch I was sitting in the cabin reading and trying not to notice the slamming of the bows on the waves when I was jerked to consciousness by an extra loud bang. I thought nothing of it for a second but then heard something scraping down the side of the boat. You have never seen anyone get out on deck so fast. An object was floating in my wake, looking as though it was a cube of concrete about 4 feet along each side. I can't imagine what it was. There didn't seem to be anything else floating around, so I went below to inspect for damage. Tins and bottles went flying as I cleared the stores from where the crash seemed to have come. To my relief, there was no sign of a leak.

This was the first, and the largest, of a number of objects I hit as I approached the American coast. The others were small pieces of wood and the occasional plastic container. I saw some large timbers but managed to avoid them, for which I was duly grateful. I think the fiber-glass hull would have survived a head-on collision, although the rigging might have snapped with the shock. More danger comes from driftwood thrown sideways into the boat in heavy weather.

"Day 41, 1400. It is very depressing to find that in spite of all my efforts I don't seem to have got very far west. And I really have no idea what my latitude is. I think the current must be stronger here than the hydrographic chart shows.

"I feel as though I am the Flying Dutchman, doomed forever to sail and never make a port."

There was a magnificent halo around the sun that afternoon, the best I have ever seen. It was eerie with its pallid spectrum. Soon clouds came up, and I knew that a frontal system was on its way. I kept my fingers crossed that it would be mild. The wind was about Force 5, and *Aziz* was hopping along like a kangaroo. I suppose the wave length was just wrong for her.

That night I felt sufficiently happy to cook myself a really magnificent macaroni Bolognese. I ate it all and felt bloated. I fancied some soda pop but had finished it all a few days earlier and had to make do with beer. I laughed at this—I could imagine the men regretting that the beer was finished and they had to drink pop.

The bad weather kept away, and by morning I was actually able to unreef the main for a Force 3 wind. Things were really looking up.

# FIFTEEN

# Nearly There

AT LAST I was making decent progress toward the right side of the Atlantic. This was Day 42, the day on which I had hoped to arrive. Before I left Britain, I had estimated that the voyage would take six weeks. This was worked out by assuming an average speed through the water of 100 miles a day and a distance through the water of 4,200 miles. This was a rather vague estimate as speed and distance would depend so much on the weather. I thought that if I were very lucky I might do it in five weeks and if I were unlucky it would take seven.

I had requested that no search be made for me until

I had been at sea for 60 days. I didn't want to cause a lot of trouble just because I had been a less successful sailor than I had hoped. Now at least I was saved that embarrassment, for I was very close, and something serious would have to happen to prevent me arriving within the next week. My noon-to-noon run was only 60 miles, but it was all in the right direction, so I felt quite confident that I would not cause too much worry to my family and friends at home.

I had a busy afternoon preparing the boat for coastal waters. The biggest job was routing out the anchors. The main anchor, a 30-pound Danforth, was stowed in the forward cabin at the far end of the berths, with the stock lying centrally between the mattresses. It was quite a business getting it out, for I had to clear away all the stores, boxes, and spare sails that were lying on top of it.

The first things out were the remaining eggs, about three dozen of them, still packed in their fragile plastic boxes. They went rapidly overboard as I was using so few that it didn't seem worth keeping more than half a dozen. They were hastily followed by several vacuum packs of bacon which my nose told me had started to putrify. Then I piled everything into the corners of the berths and wedged myself into a position where I could get hold of the anchor.

It was a real fight. I tried to lift it out, but because I was in such an awkward position I couldn't get enough leverage on it. I crawled on to the berths, my feet on the cans in the well and tried again. I got it partly out, but the crosspiece jammed under the mattress. I heaved again, and it came loose with a rush, and I nearly fell into the cans. I dragged it toward me, balanced it on the edge of the bunk, and wormed myself backward until I was standing on the main cabin floor. Finally, sweating profusely, I lifted it down and put it on the only clear floor space, just by the steps leading to the cockpit.

I then got out the 20-pound Danforth anchor from the lower stowage, a much easier job as it was a lot smaller. I took the three fathoms of chain which were on this anchor and shackled it on to the big one. Then I took the fathom of chain off the 15-pound plow anchor that was stowed in the bilge and shackled that on to the 20-pounder.

After that bit of musical chairs I got the two anchor warps from the after storage and shackled one to each anchor. Now was the opportunity to do what I had never seen done but what is always recommended: mark off the warp in lengths, so that you can tell exactly how much line is out. I did this by tying lengths of parachute cord at three-fathom intervals, and this seemed quite easy to feel as well as see.

The most entertaining job I did that day was hoisting the Dale Yacht Club burgee to the masthead. I had taken it down some time before because it was fraying, but felt that now was the time to show the flag again. I had flown the Little Ship Club burgee all the time at the starboard crosstree and it had survived, though it was decidedly tattered.

The problem in raising the burgee was that the

halyard and block were on the windward side of the mast. Each time I tried to finish hoisting, the burgee stick would either jam against the masthead fittings or under the backstay. I tried hoisting the last few feet very quickly, at the same time giving a hefty flick to windward, but without success, and after I had almost got the stick permanently stuck in the shrouds I gave up. I brought *Aziz* in to the wind, where she hung in stays until I finished the job and relatched the self-steering on course. She looked much better with the red and green burgee flying, and I felt decently dressed for any meeting with other boats.

I rewarded myself with a brandy and lemon juice. One of the advantages of having the chronometer on Greenwich Mean Time and the alarm clock on local time, about four hours earlier, was that I could justify eating or drinking at any time, as on one time or the other it was always appropriate. I had sautéed potatoes for supper, the best so far. I was now getting the hang of cooking them and felt that if I had learned nothing else from the crossing, this single skill was a worthwhile achievement.

The night was peaceful, but there were more squalls the next morning and I put a reef in the main. They can't have been too bad to warrant only one reef. Nevertheless they looked impressive. I wrote in the log "towering leaden cumulus marching across the sky trailing streamers of rain, and each bearing a tightly packed bag of wind." They soon marched away, leaving a Force 2 southwesterly breeze, and I unreefed and put on the No.

1 jib. This was the first time for ten days that I had had the No. 1 up, so I felt that things were really going well.

I managed to pick up a radio signal that I thought was from the Nantucket Shoals Light Vessel. It was faint, but the bearing was reasonable, although not accurate enough for navigation. But it was evidence that the charts were telling the truth when they said that there was land just over the horizon. "It is funny to think that I am actually going to see land in a day or two; and a land of fables and myths to me."

It rained that evening, a gentle rain like that in England instead of the spitting showers we had been having. The barometer was falling once again, and I hoped the weather wasn't going to play another nasty trick on me. I could see a lot of birds about, most of them Leach's petrels, a few storm petrels, and a number of birds which looked like black gulls.

By evening I had made enough progress to be able to get a radio DF bearing on the Nantucket Shoals Light Vessel. I got rather a shock when I plotted it.

"I seem to be way out of my navigation. According to a DF bearing on Nantucket, I am nearly 50 miles west of where I thought. Something has gone seriously wrong somewhere."

Then: "I have just taken a sight with the sun very low, but it figures well with the DF. Actually I wasn't nearly as far out as I said—I had forgotten to transfer the fix earlier today. Even so, I am a bit out, but not half as bad as I thought. At present we are about 25 miles south of the light vessel."

I was in fact only 15 miles out, which was not bad

considering the ropiness of my sextant and DF apparatus, which was all noise and not much signal. I had a terrible job taking bearings with it, as it was difficult to pinpoint the position of minimum signal strength. I think the transistors must have been passing away.

At dusk, which was at about 2300 hours GMT, I sailed about a quarter of a mile from a stationary vessel. Only when it was to windward of me did I discover to my chagrin that it was a Coast Guard vessel. I was not inclined to beat back to it for a chat, particularly as it was getting dark, but as I went quite close I thought they would have noticed me. They never did report me, which was a pity.

At about 0230 hours, in a pitch-black night, I picked up the loom of the light vessel exactly where I expected it to be—very gratifying, for I had not thought that I would be close enough to see it. I was approaching the separation lanes for shipping in and out of New York, so I spent the night having quick snatches of sleep and keeping watch. I didn't see much shipping and suspect that mist came down earlier than I realized, blocking out the lights. When light came, I could see that it was very misty, almost foggy. We were within soundings with my 30-fathom echo sounder, and the sea had changed to a cold bottle green, quite different from the warm Gulf Stream blue.

I had difficulty getting a radio bearing on the light vessel, for some reason, but was soon able to get bearings from several beacons on the coast. There was practically no wind, and I spent the day alternately drifting and trickling along. I heard on the radio station at Providence that they expected fog that night and the following morning. This was disappointing, though hardly surprising. The frequency of fog in these waters is very high.

I spent quite a time trying to make the port navigation light work, as it hadn't lit up when I asked it to the previous night. When I unscrewed the cover I discovered that the top of the bulb holder had corroded away where I had put an aluminum rivet in it shortly after buying the boat. I had to do a botch job with a spare bulb from the compass stuck up with wire and insulating tape. It worked.

Half an hour before midnight, I was surprised to see a whale playing about 300 yards away. I hadn't realized that they came into such shallow water. I was pleased to see one there, for it indicated that the water was by no means as polluted as I had been led to believe—and that the great whaling fleets of New England had not completely wiped out their victims.

I was now getting close to land, and hoped to see some sign of it before morning. I took an antisleep pill and prepared for a long night of watchkeeping and navigation.

In the middle of the night, local time, I saw a vessel heading straight for me. I couldn't make head or tail of her lights; she seemed to have them the wrong way around. She came very close, and I flashed her *D*—"keep clear, I am having difficulty maneuvering." This was an understatement, for I was completely becalmed and could not even keep *Aziz* pointing in one direction.

I heard the engines die abruptly, and she came

slowly past to have a look at me. I heard a voice exclaim with surprise, "Hey, it's a sailboat." As she came by, I could see that she was a fishing vessel, about 50 feet long, with a forward white masthead light and her red and green navigation lights on the wheelhouse sides at the rear. No wonder I had been confused; ships carry their navigation lights in front of their masthead lights.

I shouted across and asked my position and heard a surprised reaction to my voice, whether because of my woman's voice or my English accent I don't know. He did a circuit and came back to tell me that I was 10 miles due south of No Man's Land, which agreed with my estimates.

I told him that I had come nonstop from Britain and asked him to notify the Coast Guard that I was here. He had difficulty understanding me and was lost when I spelled out the name of my boat. I discovered later that Americans don't say "zed," but "zee."

The boat finally chugged off, leaving me happy knowing where I was and that I had made contact with America.

# SIXTEEN

# Discovering America

It was the most frustrating night of the voyage. The wind was light and fitful. I spent hours at the helm trying to keep *Aziz* pointing in the right direction, watching the stars spin above the mast as she drifted round and round. The surface of the water was shrouded in mist and, as the dawn broke, the sun rose dramatically from the haze, a glowing red ball, molten metal in an oily sea.

*Aziz* crept idly on in the mist while I watched the cat's paws ruffling the sea as they passed by. Shortly after dawn, I had a harbinger of land: a little green leaf beetle settled on the cabin roof and crawled inquisitively over my hand as I removed it to a safer place. Land birds flew overhead on urgent missions from island to island.

I tried to start the engine and found that the battery was too flat to turn it over. I did not have the strength to start it by hand, and if I had been able to start it I would have had to fix it permanently in gear, for the gear cable had rusted through.

At last I sighted evidence of man's presence in these foreign waters, a row of fishing buoys each with a flag hanging limply round its stick. At first I was afraid that I was close to shore, but the depth of water was still over 100 feet so I guessed that there were lobster pots below me.

The mist was quite thick now, and I could hear a foghorn calling urgently to port. I replied with my aerosol horn, deafening myself every minute. Soon a dark shape congealed from the mist, and a small ship thumped across my bows a few hundred yards away. This was my first indication of visibility in this mist, and I realized that I would have little warning of land. I thanked my lucky stars that the tides do not run strongly in this area, for I had little control of where I was going.

I spent much of the time taking radio bearings from the various beacons in the locality. The radio was so noisy that the fixes showed as large polygons on the large-scale chart. However, I was confident that I was still no closer than 10 miles from the nearest land, either Block Island or Martha's Vineyard. At about 1000 hours, local time, I was taking a set of bearings when I heard a noisy engine approaching. I popped out and saw a cabin cruiser going like a bat out of hell from west to east. I waved and brandished the loudhailer. They waved back and were soon lost in the mist.

A few minutes later I heard another engine, and out of the mist came another cabin cruiser. Again I waved and brandished my loudhailer, and the boat slowed down and came to rest close by. She was the *Edlor III* of New York, a smart cruiser about 30 feet long and, to my delight, she carried a large and businesslike radio aerial. A man and woman were aboard, and they asked me what I wanted. I explained that I was nonstop from Europe to Newport and asked that he report me to the Coast Guard, which the man did.

They asked if I needed anything, and I said, half joking, that I wouldn't mind a tow. The captain of the *Edlor* got on the radio, and after he had answered numerous questions about himself, and a few about me, the Coast Guard said they would send out a boat. They also passed the information that my parents were in Newport awaiting my arrival, which was a terrific piece of news. Before I left, they had said that they would not come to meet me since they would have no way of knowing when I would arrive. I was very pleased, knowing how much they would enjoy my success.

The *Edlor* stayed with me waiting for the Coast Guard boat. I was getting dizzy sailing round and round her, so I tied up astern and, after changing into a mini dress and tidying up a bit, went aboard. Ed Hollowell and his wife, Lorna, were on their way back to New York after a week's cruising. They gave me lunch of beer and ham and cheese sandwiches. Real bread! Even if it didn't taste like English bread I thoroughly enjoyed it. I don't know what we talked about, but I was blissfully happy.

It was odd to see *Aziz* from the outside, for she had become a part of me. She looked so large and yet so small, and I could hardly believe that she had brought me all the way from Europe. I was pleased that she was looking quite smart, apart from a few rust stains, and I congratulated her on her performance over the past six weeks.

After about an hour and a half the Coast Guard boat arrived and took me in tow. I waved goodby to the *Edlor,* and we set off at a terrific speed. I nearly had a fit, for a huge standing wave was set up with a terrific trough amidships; I feared the strain might be too great for *Aziz.* It would be a pity if she broke up now. I hooted the foghorn and explained that it was too fast, and we set off again at a more moderate pace. I took the opportunity to clear up the inside of the boat and then sat on deck, a can of beer in one hand, a cigarette in the other, and an idiot grin all over my face. I retired to the shelter of the cabin only when it started to drizzle.

After a while, we arrived close to the Brenton Reef light structure, a Meccano sculpture rising from the sea about two miles from the entrance to Narragansett Bay. The light was flashing, and the foghorn howled mournfully. I was cast adrift there and told that another boat would pick me up. The atmosphere darkened, the heavens opened, thunder cracked, and I was soaked with rain. It did not keep me from smiling happily at photographers who were firing their cameras at me from a motor boat.

Soon there appeared out of the mist a boat with a flashing blue light on top, and I was taken in tow again. We set off for the last few miles to Newport. I stood on deck waving at the photographers and the Coast Guard, my heart almost bursting with joy. Quite suddenly I realized that land was visible, a blue-gray shoreline a few hundred yards away.

I really have made it! There really is land over here. America is not an imaginary land, but a real place. Now I know how Christopher Columbus felt.

Soon more boats appeared and formed an escort. Although the rain was pouring down, I stripped off my oilskins, for the Coast Guard shouted that I was expected to be wearing hotpants. I felt that the mini dress was a good substitute for them, and stood there soaked from head to toe and enjoying every minute. A large motor yacht joined the formation, and I was told that it belonged to the Mayor of Newport.

At about four o'clock, local time, we came around a headland, and there was Newport Harbor, with plenty of yachts at anchor and moored along the quays. As we entered foghorns were sounded. A marvelous welcome for someone who had been worried that no one would be expecting her. I stood on the cabin roof, clinging to the mast, quite bemused by it all. *Aziz* was brought alongside a pontoon at the Port O' Call Marina, and there were my parents, with happy smiles on their faces.

I embraced them and helped them aboard, where we posed for photographs. Then we went below with the Customs Officer, who rapidly dealt with my passport and collected my remaining fresh fruit and vegetables, which he took away to burn. These formalities over, I stepped onto the pontoon, posed for more photographs, said a few words into a microphone, and then climbed a ramp and set foot on dry land.

I was surrounded by friendly and enthusiastic people, all asking questions. I replied as best I could, which was not very well for I was too excited to think clearly. Then my parents and I were driven to a hotel on Goat Island, where we were well looked after. It was there that I had my first of very few disappointments in America. The bathtub was too short for me to lie basking comfortably. Still, it was marvelous to soak in hot fresh water.

That evening I was feeling so fit and happy that I went to two parties and then to someone's house for delicious steak and salad. When we arrived back at the hotel at about 12:30, local time—it seemed much later to me because I was still used to Greenwich Time, which was 5:30—a television camera crew were waiting to interview me. Friends who saw the interview told me that I had already picked up an American accent. If I had, it was because I was enjoying American hospitality so much.

The next day was hectic. I spent the morning running between the two telephones in my room, answering questions, and posing for photographers. I was happy to talk to anyone and everyone, press and well-wishers. I recorded several telephone interviews with the BBC, which was fun, although after a time I found that I was saying the same thing over again.

I spent five days in Newport, and enjoyed every minute. It is a beautiful city, one of the oldest in America, and the houses have great character. The mayor, Fred Alofsin, was most hospitable. He took my parents and me around the harbor on his motor yacht and gave us a marvelous dinner at a quayside restaurant. Then he asked me to go along to a City Council meeting one evening. I went, not knowing what to expect, and was overwhelmed to be made an Honorary Citizen of Newport, and by an impressive declaration that July 26, 1971, be known henceforth as Nicolette Milnes Walker Day.

We were also well entertained by the officers of *H.M.S. Jupiter*, which was visiting Newport Naval Base. They gave me a huge Union Jack, which I flew at the masthead of *Aziz*—strictly non-etiquette, but a great show, for it was visible almost all over Newport.

The Newport Chamber of Commerce gave a champagne reception at the marina, and presented me with a splendid inscribed silver salver.

I had one worry—*Aziz*. I could not afford to have her shipped back to England, for that would cost at least £1,000, so I set about trying to sell her. Various people expressed interest, and I was hopeful that a sale could be arranged, when I received a telegram from the Esso Petroleum Company in London. They wished to buy the boat, transport her to England, and put her on display at the World Sportacular Show at Earls Court, which I was invited to open jointly with Chay Blyth, whose boat *British Steel* would also be on show. I accepted gladly, for I had not wanted to leave *Aziz* in America, far from home.

Then I received an invitation from Cunard to travel back to England as their guest on the *Queen Elizabeth*

*II*. This was great, for I wanted to travel back by sea to have another look at the ocean, this time from something big and safe. My mother and I rushed to the shops to buy clothes more suited to such a crossing than those I had brought with me.

Five days after arriving in Newport I said goodby to my parents, who were returning to England by air. I was driven across Connecticut to Westchester, the county just north of New York City, and across Westchester to Scarborough, a leafy suburb, where I was to stay with Sol Stein, who is publishing this book in America.

In Scarborough I worked with Sol on the plan for the book, trying to catch my thoughts and feelings while they were fresh. I also had time to see a little of American life. I visited the shopping center there and was amazed to discover a shop which sold twenty-some different sorts of ice cream. I was shown around the area, and was very impressed by the way the houses were tucked away among the trees. Instead of chopping the vegetation away, it had been left to enhance the attraction of the area.

I liked what I saw of America. I had found it much more attractive than I had expected, and had found the people not just chummy but genuinely friendly. I took great delight in the surprised reaction of many people when first meeting me. Clearly they expected a large, strong, horse-faced English girl, long in tooth. Instead I was small, apparently frail, round-faced—a teen-age imposter.

I visited Manhattan for a day and was amazed by it.

The chrome-plated parts were O.K., but I was staggered to see such poor housing and rotten buildings within a stone's throw of these shiny parts. I crossed on the Staten Island ferry and saw the famed Manhattan skyline, but I also saw the soupy water full of debris. But whatever the fabric of America may be like, the people I met were great. Of course, ten days is not much time to judge a place, although many commentators do with less, and I was seeing it from a rather unusual viewpoint. But I was won over from my mild British anti-Americanism, and am looking forward to my next visit.

Ten days after arriving in America, I again put out to sea—this time not alone, but in the company of about 2,000 people. Instead of a 30-foot sailing boat I was on a steam turbine-powered ocean liner 963 feet in length.

The ocean remained a child of immense power and quick temper. I was glad that I would be able to salute him, and thank him for ignoring the impertinence of my challenge. I respect the masterful Atlantic and am pleased that he respected my determination to make my voyage in pursuit of a chance of freedom.

# SEVENTEEN

# Taking the Crown

THE CROSSING on the Queen Elizabeth was my initiation into the public life I would have to face from now on. I sat on the Captain's right at dinner, which was a great honor and a pleasure for me. I was invited to many cocktail parties, where I was delighted to meet so many different people. Everyone was very kind to me, but I confess that at times I felt rather like a goldfish in a bowl, unable to hide from the surrounding eyes.

I was amused by the differing behavior of the British and American passengers. The latter would come up to me, shake my hand, and congratulate me on my achievement, but the British generally stood off, looking at me surreptitiously and muttering among themselves.

The crossing was very calm, which was a disappointment to me, though not to most of the passengers. I had hoped to see some big waves and strong winds so that I could compare them with what I had experienced in *Aziz*. The sea looked quite different from a height of 40 feet or more, crawling beneath one instead of surging around. The feeling of being a part of the ocean world was lost. Now I was only an observer, not a participator.

The liner plowed across the waters at more than 30 miles an hour, and 5½ days after leaving New York we docked in Southampton at midnight. The following morning I was faced with a press conference, which took a long time. Robin Knox-Johnston, the first man to sail nonstop round the world by himself, presented me with a reproduction painting of my boat *Aziz* on behalf of the builders, Southern Ocean Shipyard. We were photographed exhaustively, I recorded three television interviews and talked to a number of reporters.

Eventually I was free to go to a nearby hotel where the rest of the family had congregated. There were, I think, twelve of them, a small portion of my large number of relations. At last I could talk to them for a few minutes over a cup of coffee and unwind a little after the tensions of the publicity machine. Then the family scattered, returning to their respective homes, and my parents and I were driven to Newbury for lunch at my Uncle Robert's, and then back to Cheshire.

I felt then that I had really completed the round

trip and come back to where I started from. But I was not allowed to forget what I had been. A pile of letters awaited me, some congratulatory, others requesting me to attend some function or other. I determined that I should reply to everyone who wrote to me and immediately bought an electric typewriter to help me.

What I really wanted to do was to settle down and write this book, something I was looking forward to. I eventually managed to reply to all the kind people who wrote to me, and started on my writing. It was fun but hard work, although as my typing improved I was able to spend more time creating and less reproducing. Eventually I gave up writing in longhand first and took to typing straight onto the page. Ten weeks after landing in England I delivered the manuscript to the publishers.

I was not allowed to hide away to write. I was now a public figure, and as such had to attend public functions. I was rather apprehensive about this at first, but I said to myself that I must deliberately set out to enjoy these occasions, or I would suffer agonies. And I have enjoyed them. I have met a great number of interesting people and been to many interesting places.

Being a celebrity is a marvelous feeling—at first. But it involves a lot of monotonous repetition. Soon one grows tired of answering the same questions, shaking the hands of strange persons, smiling when you want to kick. It is satisfying to be honored by requests to attend dinners, give talks to important groups, appear on television. But it would be even nicer if people ceased to treat one as a freak, to come up and say, "I want to shake your hand so I can tell my friends about it," as though fame could literally rub off. If I had known when I set out all that was involved in the celebration of accomplishment, I doubt that I would have had the courage to go. But on the whole it was worth it for the satisfaction of achievement and the pleasure of being recognized as an individual. I am no longer one of the 30 million Englishwomen, or one of hundreds of industrial psychologists, or even one of four daughters. I am, at last, myself.

POWER

There are few, few indeed
Who can take the crown but keep
Integrity. Some special need
Is here required. I think a deep

Knowledge of self is first of all
Essential. Then simplicity.
Wisdom, of course, always, in call.
And there we have the mastery.

ELIZABETH JENNINGS

178

# List of Stores

## NAVIGATION

Ebbco plastic sextant
Old sextant
Harrison deck watch
Brookes and Gatehouse
   Direction Finding Radio
Brookes and Gatehouse
   Echo Sounder
Binoculars
Hand bearing compass
Dinghy compass
   (used as telltale)
Harries Protractor

Dividers
Log book
Note books
Pencils
Chinagraph pencils
Lead pencils
Ball point pens
Erasers
*Reed's Nautical Almanac*
*Air Almanac*
Sight Reduction Tables

ADMIRALTY PUBLICATIONS

*List of Lights*, vols. D, H, J.
*List of Radio Signals*, vols. II, V.
*Pilots*
   37 West Coast of England
   68 East Coast of United States, Vol. I
   59 Nova Scotia, S.E. Coast and Bay of Fundy
*Charts*
     1 Portsmouth to Canary Isles and Azores
  4409 North Atlantic Ocean—Northern portion
  1123 South Coast of Ireland to Lands End
  3272 Newfoundland to Bermuda
  2670 Cape Breton to Delaware Bay
  2860 Outer Approaches to New York
  2890 Approaches to Narragansett Bay and Buzzards Bay
  2892 Narragansett Bay

## CHANDLERY, ETC.

6 assorted blocks
Assorted shackles
Assorted snap shackles
Wood glue
Assorted thimbles
2 rigging screws
Clevis pins, split rings,
  locking wire

2 Isopon fiber-glass repair
  kits
2 sq. ft. copper sheet

Spare tiller
Various pieces of wood
Paint varnish
Silicon grease

## Appendix 1: List of Stores

10 jib hanks
2 plastic cleats
Assorted stainless steel eyes
Assorted plastic eyes
Spare battens
Length of Tufnol-type batten
    material
Sail thread
Sail cloth
Needles
Palm
Sail repair tape
Insulating tape
Plastic tape
Araldite adhesive
Evostick adhesive
2×25 fathom anchor warps
3 spinnaker sheets
Assorted mooring lines
15 fathoms 1-in. terylene line
10 fathoms 1¼-in. terylene
    line
10 fathoms ½-in. terylene
    line
Assorted thin terylene line
Assorted shock cord
Canvas bosun's chair and
    hoisting tackle
Spare bilge pump

Light oil
Plus Gas lubricating and
    protecting liquid
Combat lubricating and
    protecting liquid (aerosol)
Flexible sealer
Electric wire
Spare compass and naviga-
    tion light bulbs
Cable clips
Hose clips
2 funnels
Whipping twine
Codline
Spark plugs
Spare mainsheet
Spare jibsheet
Solar still
Tilley lamp
Assorted flashlights
Signaling lamp
Red and white smoke flares
Liferaft
Emergency radio transmitter
Aerosol foghorn
Loudhailer
Life jacket
Safety harness
Fire extinguisher

## TOOLS, ETC.

2 hammers
Assorted screwdrivers
2 wood saws
Hacksaw and blades
Midget hacksaw
Small adjustable wrench
Large adjustable wrench
2 pairs pliers
1 pair pincers
Sheet metal cutters
Wood plane
Assorted files
Assorted chisels
Pop riveter and rivets

2 hand drills
3 sets drill bits
Mole wrench
Pipe wrench
Boltcropper
Steel rule
Plug wrench
Carborundum block
Set of carving chisels
Assorted nuts, bolts and
   screws
Pocket knife
Stanley knife

## FOOD AND DRINK

9 cans steak
9 cans ground beef
10 cans meatballs
9 cans Spam
3 cans sausages
6 cans tuna
6 cans sardines
2 cans anchovies
3 cans cod roe

2 bottles cooking oil
36 pts evaporated milk
2 cans dried milk
2 lb Nescafé
100 teabags
6 lb cheese
5 dozen eggs
4 pints lemon juice
2 bottles orange squash

## Appendix 1: List of Stores

9 cans shrimp
5 cans ravioli
5 cans baked beans
5 cans curried beans
12 cans potatoes
10 cans assorted vegetables
15 cans assorted fruit
1 can ham
2 cans asparagus
1 can lichees
9 pkts Surprise peas
9 pkts Surprise beans
4 tubs dried vegetable flakes
9 dehydrated meals
12 pkts instant potato
1 lb spaghetti
3 lb quick macaroni
5 lb rice
3 lb flour
3 pkts oatmeal
5 lb black bread
10 lb sugar
5 lb dried fruit
5 lb canned butter
2 lb lard

Assorted sauces, pickles,
    herbs, and spices
2 jars marmalade
2 jars jam
2 jars honey
2 jars Marmite
10 pkts Ryvita
2 tins biscuits
Mother's biscuits and cake
4 lb muesli
10 cans soup
10 pkts soup
10 lb potatoes
10 lb onions
5 lb carrots
4 doz oranges
2 doz apples
5 lemons
1 box green tomatoes
6 dozen cans beer
6 bottles whisky
6 bottles brandy
12 bottles carbonated drinks
1,000 cigarettes
4 lb sweets

## MISCELLANEOUS

Radio
2 cassette tape recorders

2 Cameras
Film

5 recorded music tapes
5 unused tapes
Approx. 40 assorted books
Sewing kit
Washing kit
Soap
Liquid detergent
Disinfectant
Shampoo
Toilet paper
Paper towels
Clothespins
2 alarm clocks

Fishing tackle
Matches
Tea towels
2 prs. scissors
Vanity case with cosmetics,
   etc.
2 frying pans
1 non-stick saucepan
1 pressure cooker
1 kettle
Assorted crockery and
   cutlery

# The Boat

*Aziz* IS A Pionier class fast cruiser racer. This class was designed by E. G. Van de Stadt in 1959, one of the first yachts designed specifically to be built of fiber glass. The class proved successful both in offshore racing and for cruising, and over two hundred were built by Southern Ocean Shipyard Ltd. of Poole, Dorset.

    *Aziz* is the thirty-ninth Pionier and was built in 1963 for the late Captain Jack Sanderson of Budleigh Salterton, Devon, who was a polo player well known in both India and England. The name is Arabic and means magnificent or beautiful, and the boat was called after Captain Sanderson's favorite polo pony.

In 1969 *Aziz* was sold to Mr. Ric Carpenter of Cowes, Isle of Wight, who used her for channel cruising.

I bought *Aziz* from Mr. Carpenter in March 1971. She was in good condition and had clearly been well looked after. No major repairs were necessary.

The diagrams show her sail plan, accommodation layout and dimensions.

I had four major modifications made: two to strengthen the structure and two to ease single-handed sailing.

The windows, which are six feet long without a break in the plastic, were covered with plywood boards into which were set plastic portholes. I had this done because I felt that so long a window might be vulnerable if the boat were thrown on her beam ends. The after bulkhead was strengthened by the addition of solid teak beams as Brian Henshall, of the Dale Sailing Company, thought that they might not stand up to a pooping sea. The washboards were also reinforced.

A Hasler Gibbs servo pendulum self-steering gear was fitted. This involved the manufacture of a bracket to support the vane, as *Aziz* was not fitted with a stern pulpit. This bracket was made by Dick Edwards of Dale from 1½-inch galvanized pipe and proved quite satisfactory.

Before collecting *Aziz* from Cowes, I had a twin forestay fitted. This was to allow me to carry twin foresails when sailing downwind, and to allow me to keep one foresail hanked on ready for use. As it happened, I rarely did this as I always seemed to have the wrong sail hanked on.

The internal arrangements were quite satisfactory, and for one person there was plenty of space.

My only complaints about the design of the boat are that the forehatch was badly secured and leaked despite being sealed all around. Because the attachment was in the center of the circular hatch cover, the cover itself was quite noticeably deformed. I would also have liked a spray rail on the cabin roof. Frequently a wave would come over the bows, up over the roof, and drop into the cabin.

As regards sails, I had little to complain about. I was glad that I had acquired an extra jib to fill the gap between the working and storm jibs. It was very useful. I also think that the storm jib was too large; about 40 square feet would have been better.

All the gear worked well, and the only breakages I had were a shroud and the starboard jib fairlead slide. I had no difficulty handling the gear, but could not have managed without two mast winches. That for the main halyard was essential when unreefing the mainsail.

*APPENDIX 3*

# Facts and Figures

**ROUTE**

I chose to go by the Azores route as I was making the crossing for pleasure and not in a race. The direct route, in my opinion, is more dangerous as well as more uncomfortable. It takes one along the shipping lanes, across the Grand Banks with their fog and fishing fleets, and down the Canadian coast. The Azores route is away from shipping, warmer and less windy, and does not involve any long coastal passage.

I divided the route into three parts.

Part 1. The Great Circle route from St. Ann's Head

to a point between São Miguel and Terceira in the Azores, continued to latitude 37° N.

Part 2. Due West along latitude 37° N. until reaching longitude 65° W. This is just south of the Gulf Stream flow.

Part 3. From 65° W. a Great Circle route to Rhode Island. This allows one to cross the strong flow of the Gulf Stream where it is fairly narrow.

I did not follow this plan exactly because of weather and poor tactics. I allowed myself to get too far east of course on Part 1, and passed between São Miguel and Santa Maria because I did not want to beat into the westerly wind to get north of São Miguel. I now think it would have been better if I had done so.

In Part 2, I allowed myself to get a little far north early on, which meant I had difficulty in staying out of the Gulf Stream flow. As I approached the end of this part I allowed myself to be pushed into the Gulf Stream a bit too soon, and in the ensuing bad weather drifted east so that my course to cross the Stream was less oblique than I wanted. This meant that the current had a greater effect than it would otherwise have had.

Despite starting Part 3 from the wrong place I was able to make a good course toward land and made my landfall without trouble.

I reckoned that the divergencies from my plan cost me between two and five days. I would not change the planned route another time.

NAVIGATION

I had trouble with my sextant early on and was uncertain of my position until I picked up the Azores beacons on the radio. I discovered that the index error on the sextant was continually changing, and had to measure it each time I took a sight. After that I had no problems, and I think that my navigation gave fixes within fifteen miles of my true position at worst.

I had great difficulty in using the radio Direction Finding set because there was so much hiss and crackle coming through the headphones that I could not hear the signal clearly. I should have had it serviced before I set out.

The Harrison deck watch that I was using as a chronometer was a bit erratic, but I was able to pick up time signals from the British or Australian broadcasting services nearly every day.

The rotating log worked well until toward the end of the crossing when the clock part seemed to stiffen up so that the line would wind itself up before spinning the clock "winder." I was about to oil it when I accidentally cut off the rotator, so did not bother.

The echo sounder gave me no trouble and was very useful when I was approaching land in fog.

SPEED AND DISTANCE

Distance over the ground: 3,400 nautical miles.
Average speed over the ground: 76½ miles per day.
Distance through the water: 4,000 n. miles.*
Average speed through the water: 90 miles per day.*

* Estimated as the log rotator was lost late in the voyage.

# Appendix 3: Facts and Figures

Greatest day's run recorded on the log: 137 n. miles.
Greatest day's run noon-to-noon by sights: 158 n. miles.*
Smallest day's run recorded on the log: 28 n. miles.
Smallest day's run noon-to-noon by sights: 34 n. miles.
(But also note 88 n. miles in three days during the Gulf Stream bad weather.)

SAIL CHANGES
Total mainsail changes (reefing and unreefing): 65.
Total headsail changes (including removing but not replacing a sail): 59.

USAGE OF HEADSAILS

| Genoa | Small Genoa | No. 1 jib | No. 2 jib | No. 3 jib | Storm jib |
|-------|-------------|-----------|-----------|-----------|-----------|
| 9 | 1 | 18 | 10 | 13 | 6 |

* Probably an overestimate, but some bonus from current gained.